"We're told in Scripture that God loves those who give cheerfully, which means the way we approach donors needs to nurture this emotion. And this book shows just how to do that—establish a resource development program that yields transformed hearts and generous gifts. What a difference it would make if every ministry would put this into practice."

John Ashmen, President,
Association of Gospel Rescue Missions

"The basic premise of *The Sower*—that growing givers' hearts should be a priority for the fundraising programs of Christian ministries—is a message that today's hard-pressed fundraisers need to hear and practice. It's a challenge to balance the very real financial needs of our organizations with the spiritual nurture of donors, but as the authors suggest, the resulting eternal fruit makes doing so well worth the effort. I commend this book to persons and ministries who are serious about raising resources in a God-honoring way."

Rebekah Burch Basinger,
Executive Director for Congregational Relations,
Brethren in Christ Church of North America

"Scott Rodin and Gary Hoag are unique individuals. They are trained New Testament scholars and experienced seminary executives and fundraisers. When they team up for this booklet, the result is a thoroughly biblical approach to ministering to donors and potential donors that seeks to transform them into whole-life stewards for God in Christ, whether it benefits the fundraiser's organization or not. Not surprisingly, more often than not it does! A must read."

Craig Blomberg, Ph.D., Distinguished Professor
of New Testament, Denver Seminary

"The triune God of the Christian faith is distinct from all other so-called gods in that He is the God of generous giving and sharing. God the Father has given generously His only beloved Son for sinners, who are His enemies. This book exhorts all true disciples of Jesus Christ to participate in the life of faithful stewardship and generous giving with the power of the Holy Spirit. This is a must reading for all Christians in the whole globe who are struggling everyday to imitate the character of the triune God."

Sung Wook Chung, D.Phil. (Oxford University), Pastor, Professor and Bestselling Korean Author

"I am encouraged to see this quality publication that defines development work as ministry in the Kingdom of God that replaces manipulative transactional techniques and closing strategies with a dependence on prayer and relationship-building as the essential tools for success. The authors call us to our appropriate roles to sow faithfully, and then wait and hope and believe. Sowers cannot play God and cause the seeds to grow. All they can do, and must do, is sow faithfully and regularly and trust God for the increase."

Howard Dayton, President, Compass—Finances God's Way, Cofounder, Crown Financial Ministries

"Ministries can use all the help they can get to understand how to raise money from a biblical worldview. The Sower does a wonderful job of being both theologically sound and practical in application to help ministries honor God in how they raise Kingdom resources."

Melinda Delahoyde, President, Care Net

"Funding the vision of the Great Commission is spiritual work that must be done in ways that places a priority on developing better stewards of Kingdom resources. This book will help you do just that."

Steve Moore, President & CEO,
The Mission Exchange

"Scott and Gary understand that the primary motivation of an effective asker is not the liberation of resources but the liberation of people. They practically explain how, as people are liberated, resources can be liberated exponentially. I encourage you to read and apply this book for the benefit of the asker, the giver, and the Kingdom!"

Todd Harper, President,
Generous Giving

"Scott Rodin and Gary Hoag are respected stewardship learners and leaders. This book takes Christian leaders, staff, volunteers, and givers on a journey that will transform their thinking, fundraising, giving, and generosity. This is a must-read for anyone who wants to go deeper and go further in their generosity journey."

Brian Kluth, Author, Radio Speaker,
Founder of Maximum Generosity

"There is a generosity movement afoot in this country as God is working in the hearts and minds of ministry leaders, pastors and givers to understand the joy of generosity. This book is an excellent resource to help the reader understand the blessedness that God wants for each of us as we seek to live the generous life. Scott and Gary are wise guides into this blessed life. I highly recommend that you listen to them!"

Patrick Johnson, Vice President Churches,
The National Christian Foundation

"While we clearly know that ministry requires money, many of us struggle with the whys and the hows of raising money for God's Kingdom purposes. This book sets forth a helpful definition of development work as a ministry in and of itself—and in so doing—empowers God's people to do the work to which He has called them."

Elisa Morgan, President Emerita,
MOPS International, Publisher, FulFill™

"Out of my personal experience in raising resources for over 20 years in Christian ministry, I fully concur with the basic premises of this book that generous giving is not the result of a ministry's work, but God's work in people; that true generosity flows from transformed hearts as they are conformed to the image of Christ who is generous; and that Christian fundraising is not merely about marketing transactions to secure gifts but it is about encouraging spiritual transformation, which is helping people become rich toward God through their giving."

Adam Morris, Ph.D., Vice President Advancement,
Biola University

"Our thoughts about raising resources for the cause of Christ have needed an overhaul for years. At last, Scott and Gary refocus our minds and hearts on celebrating God as our sole Provider and they've redefined the role of "asking" in a wonderfully biblical way. This book is a much-needed help to all of us who have been called to the ministry of cultivating stewards whose hearts desire to be rich toward God."

Joseph M. Stowell, Ph.D, President,
Cornerstone University

"Tired of raising money and wish you could focus on developing people who love God and give generously out of their love relationship? Rodin and Hoag provide a thoroughly biblical foundation and reorientation for our approach to fundraising. They show us that God wants us to stop focusing on raising money and to start discipling people to become godly stewards. Additionally, this book is filled with wise, practical advice for how to make this shift. The distinction between God's role and our responsibilities will set you free and allow you to discover what could become the most meaningful season of our work."

G. Craig Williford, Ph.D., President,
Trinity International University

"The topic of helping people become rich toward God through their generosity is close to my heart and this booklet is a great addition to the material available. Both givers and those who seek to influence them will find this an encouraging, practical and thoroughly biblical resource."

David Wills, President,
The National Christian Foundation

THE
SOWER

Redefining *the* Ministry *of* Raising Kingdom Resources

R. SCOTT RODIN & GARY G. HOAG

www.SowerBook.org

Cover: Sower with Setting Sun, Vincent Van Gogh

Scripture quotations are from the New International Version of the Bible.

© 2010 ECFAPress

ISBN-10: 0-9799907-9-3
ISBN-13: 978-0-9799907-9-3

The Authors

R. Scott Rodin is the Managing Principal of OneAccord NFP. He leads a national team of proven professionals who combine their skills and experience to help transform nonprofit organizations through professional partnership. Their two-fold commitment is to speak absolute truth with absolute compassion, and their mission is to help nonprofit organizations, ministries, and churches increase revenue, improve effectiveness and make successful transitions in leadership to fulfill their mission and realize their vision. Dr. Rodin holds a Ph.D. in Theology from the University of Aberdeen, Scotland. He is a Senior Fellow of the Engstrom Institute, and is the former president of the Christian Stewardship Association and Palmer Theological Seminary. He is the author of seven books including, *Stewards in the Kingdom, The Seven Deadly Sins of Christian Fundraising*, and *The Steward Leader*.

Gary Hoag has been encouraging Christian generosity for more than 20 years serving in leadership positions at Denver Seminary, Colorado Christian University and Biola University. He grew up in a Christian home where generosity was a way of life, earned a B.A. in business from Cedarville College, received an M.Div. at Talbot School of Theology, and was ordained as a minister with the Evangelical Free Church at St. Jude's Anglican Cathedral in Canada. Hoag launched Generosity Monk in 2009 because he believes God has called him to dedicate his life to encouraging Christian generosity by providing spiritual and strategic counsel. He contributed a chapter to *Revolution in Generosity* and served as a content reviewer for the NIV Stewardship Study Bible. Hoag is currently working on a Ph.D. in New Testament on the Rich and their Relationship with Riches in 1 Timothy at Trinity College, in Bristol, UK. Hoag resides in Colorado with his wife, Jenni, and two children, Sammy and Sophie.

Table of Contents

Foreword

From the beginning of the formative years of ECFA, the ideas suggested and processes put in place (such as the standards and best practices) have been based on a biblical worldview that relies on the truth of God's word as the authority. The basis for this position is found in 2 Corinthians 8:21 (NIV): "For we are taking pains to do what is right, not only in the eyes of the Lord but also in the eyes of man." As you look at the ECFA standards, there are three basic areas that constitute the concerns of accountability: governance, finances and fundraising/stewardship. This book concerns itself with this third area and is addressed, in particular, to all those in ministry that desire to raise resources from a biblical worldview.

This publication is actually an extension of many previous steps ECFA has taken to provide resources in this area. Many Christian ministries had been using secular fundraising techniques with little attention given to whether the practices were consistent with God's word. In 2003, ECFA joined in an effort to look at a biblical worldview for raising resources. A taskforce of 23 individuals (including three seminary presidents) were assembled under the leadership of Wesley K. Willmer (then a vice president at Biola University). As a result of this group's work, it developed the Biblical Principles of Stewardship and Fundraising document (see Appendix B). ECFA published these principles which were some of the early documents to advance a biblically-based movement that looks at the primary purpose of fundraising as raising people to be rich toward God. As a further development of these principles, this book is based on these three assumptions:

1. **Generous giving is not predicated solely on the work of an individual or an organization's efforts, but rather on God's work in people.** As you will read, the foundational Scripture for this book, 1 Corinthians 3:6-9, reminds us that though we sow and cultivate in people's lives and may have the privilege of reaping, God is the one who makes things grow. This truth and the other

ideas in this book are designed to change your organization's whole perspective on raising Kingdom resources.

2. **Generosity flows from transformed hearts as they conform to the image of Christ, who is generous.** Scripture shows us the stark contrast between the true generosity of Barnabas (Acts 4:32-37) and the imitation generosity of Ananias and Sapphira (Acts 5:1-11). The premise of this book is that to encourage Christian generosity, you must intentionally sow spiritual seed in the lives of God's people. This book will show your ministry whether it has any seed to sow, and if not, how to fill your seed bags.

3. **Christian resource-raising is not solely about securing transactions or gifts; rather it is about encouraging spiritual transformation—helping people become givers rich toward God.** In Philippians 4:17, the Apostle Paul said, "Not that I am looking for a gift, but I am looking for what may be credited to your account." Paul cared about what was happening in the hearts and lives of the Christians in Philippi regardless of whether or not they gave. This book will instruct you in how to accomplish this in your own life and work.

It is my earnest prayer that God will use this book in a significant way to raise, from a biblical worldview, the necessary resources to fulfill the Great Commission.

Dan Busby
President
ECFA

Preface

In *Finding God in Unexpected Places*, Philip Yancey recalls how he saved every fundraising appeal he received for a month's time and then analyzed the 62 appeals. As a result, he concluded that appeals from Christian organizations used the same transactional techniques (underlining, use of P.S., focus on urgency, etc.) as everyone else and that not a single appeal from a Christian organization focused on Yancey's need as a Christian to honor and obey God through his giving. Similarly, Denver Seminary Distinguished Professor of New Testament Craig Blomberg in the book, *Revolution in Generosity*, raises the core issue: why is it that "Christian ministries that are raising money do not stress the central biblical truths that giving is a part of whole-life transformation, that stewardship and sanctification go together as signs of Christian obedience and maturity, and that God will call us to account for what we do with 100 percent of the possessions He has loaned us."

Both Yancey and Blomberg are correct—that most Christian ministries have adopted the "whatever works" approach of the transactional science of most fundraising. However, generosity is not happening when the general population is giving barely one percent per capita and the most generous group—evangelicals—are barely giving four percent per capita. In general, Christians want to avoid the topic of faith and finances. Most seminaries are not teaching on the topic and pastors are avoiding it like the plague. As a result, fundraisers from Christian organizations have joined the path of our culture in raising resources. So a crisis exists, a lack of generosity due to denying that wise stewardship and generous giving are the natural outcome of a life devoted to God and Christ, and that it is through God's transforming a person's heart to reflect the image of Christ that he or she becomes generous as Christ is generous. We must shift our focus from asking to helping Christians be rich toward God by honoring God with their possessions.

Scott Rodin and Gary Hoag address these concerns for the lack of generosity and the concerns for the lack of spiritual focus by Philip Yancey and Craig Blomberg by providing a redefinition of how resources should be raised within Christian ministries. *The Sower* outlines both the theological tenets of how money should be raised from a biblical worldview and also provides practical steps to apply these principles to ongoing ministry efforts.

The message in this book is not found many other places. One of the book's strengths is the unique experience of the authors. Both Scott Rodin and Gary Hoag have been trained theologically and they both have worked in practical resource development assignments. As a result, this is not just pie-in-the-sky scholarly writing, but rather that the values of the authors have been successfully field tested over time as practitioners. I believe this book is a resource that you will want to continue referring back to as you try to focus on how God would have you honor Him in your fundraising efforts.

The cover art of this books tells a vivid story about some of the central themes of this publication. While the role of those in raising resources is to sow and water seeds, God alone is the One Who makes things to grow (I Cor. 3:1-9). We need to keep this in mind. God is the One Who raises funds. In addition, the image of the sower and the setting sun captures the state of the Church today. Time may be short before Christ returns, so we must sow biblical principles with a level of urgency. The birds represent the evil one that may steal the seed you sow, but that must not stop us from raising resources from God's perspective.

Horace Bushnell is credited with saying, "One more revival, only one more is needed; the revival of Christian stewardship; the consecration of the money power of the Church unto God; and when that revival comes, the Kingdom of God will come in a day. You can no more prevent it than you can hold back the tides of the ocean." Perhaps if everyone sowed as God calls us to, we could bring on that revival of Christian stewardship that could make the Kingdom of God come in a day. I encourage you to read on and join the movement of becoming a faithful sower.

Wesley K. Willmer, Ph.D.
Senior Vice President
ECFA

Introduction

This book was written to provide momentum for a movement aimed at the heart of every person involved in the process of raising resources or giving money for the work of God's Kingdom. You may be a full-time development officer, an executive director, a pastor, a president, a board member, a volunteer or a faithful giver. You may have decades of experience in fund development or this may be the first thing you have ever read on this topic. Regardless, if you care about giving or raising resources for God's work using a biblical perspective, this book is written for you.

The movement we are supporting is an effort to move away from the commonly used transactional approach to raising money and toward a more biblical approach of transforming hearts. Put a different way, it is realigning priorities to place changed hearts toward God above changed bank balances. It is a new order that seeks to develop faithful stewards whose hearts are rich toward God. It redefines development work as ministry in the Kingdom of God. And it replaces manipulative techniques and closing strategies with a dependence on prayer and relationship-building as the essential tools for success.

For too long there has been too little said about how we should be raising money in the Kingdom of God. Secular approaches were adopted without question by Christian organizations and ministries. As a result, while we may have had some success in raising money, we have failed to raise up godly stewards. In the past several years, however, the silence has been broken; a wide range of voices has joined with a small group of long-time faithful advocates to call our practices into question. The result of these combined forces is a movement among Christian development professionals, consultants, theologians and ministry leaders to re-think our entire approach to raising money for God's work.

When we set out to put this book together, we searched for a word picture to convey simply the ideas we sought to present. We found one in the text below from Paul's first letter to the Corinthians. Facing division in the church between camps that preferred one style of leadership and teaching over another, Paul used an agricultural metaphor to exhort the church to unity. Hear what he says in 1 Corinthians 3:1-9:

> Brothers, I could not address you as spiritual but as worldly—mere infants in Christ. I gave you milk, not solid food, for you were not yet ready for it. Indeed, you are still not ready. You are still worldly. For since there is jealousy and quarreling among you, are you not worldly? Are you not acting like mere men? For when one says, "I follow Paul," and another, "I follow Apollos," are you not mere men? What, after all, is Apollos? And what is Paul? Only servants, through whom you came to believe—as the Lord has assigned to each his task. I planted the seed, Apollos watered it, but God made it grow. So neither he who plants nor he who waters is anything, but only God, who makes things grow. The man who plants and the man who waters have one purpose, and each will be rewarded according to his own labor. For we are God's fellow workers; you are God's field, God's building.

Paul clarifies and defines his vocation in relationship to God's work. He diverts all praise and glory away from himself and Apollos and gives it solely to God for the ministry that has taken place in Corinth. He will not allow himself, Apollos, or those who follow them to steal glory from God. They each have a role to play, but compared to God's work of "making things grow," Paul's and Apollos' work of planting and watering amounts to very little. This is not meant to demean our work, but to place it in its proper relationship to the work of God in and through (and sometimes in spite of) ours.

So Paul plants. This is a noble and holy vocation, and it is essential for crops to grow. God does not rain down heavenly seed. Crops need a sower. In spiritual terms, people need leaders to instruct, admonish, and exhort them. All of God's people are in a process of growing in discipleship and service. Sowers plant seeds to foster that growth.

All of us who profess faith in Christ have sowers in our lives. Some are pastors, some teachers, some mentors, some family members, some colleagues, some spouses and some children. Likewise, many of us are sowing seed in the lives of others.

There is an interesting aspect to sowing seed. For all of its importance in the possibilities for growth, it has a distinct limit and requires a deep faith. The limit is simply that once the seed is in the ground, the sower has no more control over what happens. Good seed on good ground should produce a good crop, but does not necessarily. Possibly you have experienced planting potatoes in a lovely box with good earth, fertilizer, and plenty of water. Nearby is a compost pile where kitchen waste was thrown, including peelings and old potatoes that had gone bad. Several weeks after sowing the potatoes, a nasty bug got into the potato plants and destroyed them, while over in our compost pile, a rotten potato sprouts into a healthy plant, growing happily in the rubbish. Go figure!

All that sowers can do is sow faithfully. Then they have to wait and hope and believe. Sowers cannot play God and cause the seeds to grow. All they can do, and must do, is sow faithfully and regularly, and trust God for the increase.

For this reason, the image of the faithful sower is the perfect thesis of this book. Part I – The Calling of the Sower lays out a biblical foundation for raising up more than money in the Kingdom of God. Part II – The Seasons of Work for the Sower provides a framework organized as a farmer's almanac for applying these concepts to our calling as askers and givers. The goal of these two sections is to demonstrate that sowers raise more than resources for Kingdom work. Sowers raise up stewards to be rich toward God.

PART I

The Calling
of the Sower

R. Scott Rodin

The sole purpose for sowing seeds is to nurture growth. The desire for growth in spiritual terms is at the heart of what it means to be a Christian. As followers of Jesus Christ, all of us are on a journey, and that journey involves continual growth. As we grow in faith, trust and submission, in service and devotion, we journey farther along the road to which God has called us. Growing and journeying are integrally related.

A disciple's journey is made up of specific movements that shift us away from some things and toward others. For example, we are on a journey from brokenness to wholeness; we all seek the full restoration of the relationships in our lives. We are on a journey from separation to intimacy; God is calling every one of us to a deeper intimacy with Him. We are on a journey from disobedience to faithfulness; God is calling us to ever more and more faithfulness in our relationship with Him. And we are on a journey from self-reliance to submission and trust. These are just a few examples of the areas of growth in the life of each steward.

This journey begins with faith in Jesus Christ, and from there it is a lifetime of journeying toward wholeness and intimacy and faithfulness and submission and trust. If you believe that you are on that journey as a child of God, it is important to understand that everyone involved in your ministry is on that same journey. That includes your givers! If they are believers, they are walking that same path. This should impact the way we pray for them, the way we seek to interact with them, and the way we talk with them about their resources. In the same way we rely on others to spread seed into our lives that we may grow, we must understand our calling to do the same for those around us, including our supporters.

We need each other on this journey because God works through His people. We do not go on this journey alone. God organizes us into families, churches, communities, and into the body of Christ. We are intended to journey together in relationship, just as God created us, because God values relationships. If you have been a faithful giver or have worked in development very long, you know the value and the importance of relationships. Remember, the people you interact with are on that journey too; your boss is on that journey, your co-workers are on the journey, your board of directors is on that journey, and we are called and commanded to journey together. For us as authors, understanding the journey is the fundamental operating system of our development work.

Every movement from one place to another along the path that God desires us to walk is the result of growth. And that growth is most often the product of seed sown in our lives. Without people spreading seed, the growth of the Body of Christ stagnates. Stagnation means we cease to move along the pathways that mark our walk with Jesus Christ.

Are you growing or stagnating in your journey? Where do the seeds come from that make growth possible in your life? Find the sowers in your life and cultivate those relationships. They are vital to your walk with Christ.

On the other side, are you sowing seeds into the lives of the people you care about? Are the people in your life growing? Ask that question directly of your spouse, your children, your boss, your co-workers, your fellow parishioners, your friends and your financial supporters. Are you sowing good seed in their lives to help them grow?

The calling of the sower requires us to: (1) shift from transactions to transformation, (2) move from two-kingdom bondage to one-Kingdom freedom, (3) focus on cultivating hearts that will joyously become stewards, and (4) grow as a sower.

Shift from Transactions to Transformation

"O man, send your treasure on, send it ahead into heaven,
or else your God-given souls will be buried in the earth.
Gold comes from the depth of the earth—
the soul, from the highest heaven.
Clearly it is better to carry the gold to where the soul resides
than to bury the soul in the mine of the gold.
That is why God orders those who will serve in his army
here below to fight as men stripped of concern for riches
and unencumbered by anything.
To these he has granted the privilege of reigning in heaven."[1]

 Peter Chrysologus (c. 380-450)

In 1 Samuel 15, Samuel rebukes King Saul for not listening to God before going to war with the Amalekites. Starting at verse 20, Saul replies to Samuel,

> "But I did obey the Lord," Saul said, "I went on the mission the Lord assigned me. I completely destroyed the Amalekites and brought back Agag their king. The soldiers took sheep and cattle from the plunder, the best of what was devoted to God, in order to sacrifice them to the Lord your God at Gilgal."

Remember that Saul was told to destroy the Amalekites and not bring anything back. But Saul thought he had a better plan. He decided to bring back the very best of the livestock and flocks, sacrifice some to God, and keep the rest to add to his own herds and flocks. So, after disobeying God, he returned, believing that he could appease God by sacrificing a few of the best animals to Him.

Samuel would have none of it. He rebuked Saul, saying, "Does the Lord delight in burnt offerings and sacrifices as much as in obeying the voice of the Lord? To obey is better than sacrifice, and to heed is better than the fat of rams."

To obey is better than sacrifice. Hold that thought for a minute and let's look at Hosea chapter 6 starting at verse 6, "For I desire mercy, not sacrifice, and acknowledgement of God rather than burnt offerings. Like Adam, they have broken the covenant—they were unfaithful to me there." Hosea is calling out to the children of Israel saying, "God is tired of sacrifices, He is not looking for sacrifices, He wants mercy."

Finally, let's turn to the great text from the first chapter of the book of Isaiah. Isaiah continues on the same theme, starting at verse 10,

> Hear the word of the Lord, you rulers of Sodom, listen to the law of our God, you people of Gomorrah! 'The multitude of your sacrifices—what are they to me?' says the Lord. 'I have more than enough burnt offerings of the rams and the fat of fattened animals, I have no pleasure in the blood of bulls and lambs and goats. When you come to appear before me, who has asked this of you, this trampling of my courts? Stop bringing meaningless offerings! Your incense is detestable to me. New moons, Sabbaths, and convocations—I cannot bear your evil assemblies. Your new moon festivals and your appointed feasts my soul hates. They have become a burden to me; I am weary of bearing them. When you spread out your hands in prayer, I will hide my eyes from you; even if you offer many prayers, I will not listen. Your hands are full of blood; wash and make yourselves clean. Take your evil deeds out of my sight! Stop doing wrong, learn to do right! Seek justice, encourage the oppressed. Defend the cause of the fatherless, plead the case of the widow.'

What does this have to do with the journey from transaction to transformation? I believe that throughout Scripture, God is constantly calling us to examine the outward work that we do in relation to the heart we have in doing that work. The children of Israel were doing the right things. They were carrying out rituals just as God had called them to do. God set up the Levitical priesthood, the temple, the sacrificial system, and His people were going through the outward motions just as instructed. However, their hearts were far from God. Saul assumed wrongly that a simple external act of sacrifice would atone for his disobedience. Hosea lamented that, among the children of Israel, burnt offerings had been substituted for an acknowledgement of God. They were doing right techniques, they were practicing things that worked, but their hearts were somewhere else. And God grew tired of it.

In the New Testament we find the same disconnect between hearts and hands. Consider the story of Mary and Martha. Jesus comes to visit Bethany. Martha gets busy in the kitchen, *doing* all the right things. Mary forsakes the doing and goes to sit at Jesus' feet, and Martha is not happy. Mary is not *doing* the work she is supposed to do. She appears to be wasting her time sitting at the feet of Jesus and listening to His words. Yet Jesus commends Mary for making the better choice.

From nearly fifty years combined working with ministries, we have concluded that we, like Martha, are *doing* ourselves to death. Every single one of you reading this can *do* yourself to the point of exhaustion, burnout, discouragement and despair. There is enough to do in your ministry to totally consume you and spit you out. Do you agree? And yet many of you are being pressured to do still more because more money needs to be raised. There is more financial pressure on ministries today, which means we have got to be asking more, talking to more givers, securing more gifts, getting our president in front of people more often, involving our board more, and on and on. Am I on the right track? We are all feeling it, and it is all about *doing*.

More than any other area of ministry today, we are measured in this work by what we do. The *development* department makes its reports using charts and graphs. We talk about our work in terms of dollar goals, percentages of participation, average gifts and pledge totals. From thermometers in lobbies to annual reports mailed to our entire databases, everybody knows exactly if we are successful or not. Ours is a highly measurable profession where we are evaluated almost solely on what we do and how much we raise. There is something fundamentally wrong with this picture.

Think back to our image of the sower; it is as if we are being asked to both sow *and* make things grow. We are responsible for not only planting seed and watering, but also for the crop and the harvest. Indeed, in this understanding of our work, the image of the sower is inadequate. Organizations want harvesters, believing that we control the crops. Paraphrasing Paul, we have built our fundraising programs on the belief that "the president plants, the volunteers water, and the development department brings the increase." Where is God in this? Where indeed!

To change this way of thinking requires nothing short of a revolution. And the movement we spoke of is the thunder in the distance alerting us that revolution is coming.

This brings us to three fundamental statements about this journey and our role as sowers. First, *God is primarily concerned with who we are rather than what we do.* That is a life-changing statement. God is passionate about you becoming a more deeply committed child of God, because He knows that as you become more like Christ, your life will be transformed from the inside out.

If you believe this statement, let's look at how well that priority is reflected in your daily schedule. Does your work life reflect God's priority of forming and shaping you to be a child of God that you might do the work of the Kingdom? How about your devotional life? How much time are you spending intimately in the Word of God, in prayer, in devotion? In what ways do you make yourself available daily for God to take you on the journey of the transformation of your heart?

We all need sowers to help us, and we all need to be sowing in the lives of others. One truth must guide us here. We cannot sow if we are not growing. Spiritually stagnated people have empty seed bags. As followers of Christ, we must be growing daily so that our seed bags will be full. As those entrusted with the calling to raise money for God's work, we must be faithful sowers of good seed in the lives of our co-workers, our volunteers and our givers.

The second statement that flows from the first one is this: *God is primarily concerned with our being before our doing.* As mentioned, we are doing ourselves to death. Very few people could be accused of spending so much time developing their characters as children of God that they aren't doing anything for the Kingdom. In fact, I don't know anybody guilty of spending too much time *being* with God. People who spend an inordinate amount of time developing their hearts and characters as children of God are *doing* some pretty amazing things. They are people in balance; people who prioritize *being* before *doing*.

How do you find that balance in a job that is measured solely by *doing*? That is the challenge we face, and we must fight that battle first on a personal level. Restoring the balance between *being* and *doing* is the most critical responsibility of any worker in God's Kingdom. The enemy will deceive us into thinking that God desires our *doing* first, even at the expense of our *being*.

I served as a seminary president for five years. One story that deeply troubled me was hearing that students considered their seminary years as among the spiritually driest times of their lives. It seemed impossible, surrounded by libraries full of classics of the faith, professors who were deeply mature and committed followers of Christ, and a curriculum that led them through the best thinking on the Christian faith and life. Their explanation was simple and disturbing: their focus for four years was on *doing* at the expense of *being*. They worked so hard to do the work of learning about God, about the church, and about ministry that they crowded out all time for being with God Himself. How many pastors, ministry leaders and, yes, development officers have the same regret? How many of us enter each day with empty seed bags? Once again, we cannot sow what we do not have, and what replenishes our seed bags is not our doing but our being; our availability to the Holy Spirit to move us to deeper faith, richer fellowship and greater understanding. Apart from the Spirit working in us in our quiet, intimate, and surrendered moments with God, we will cease to be sowers.

Maintaining this balance will also likely require you to fight this battle in your place of work. In a system that expects a harvester, you may have to do battle in your institution to be allowed to maintain the role of the sower. What does that balance look like to you in your personal life, your family life, your marriage and your work life? Is your *"being"* being sacrificed on the altar of deadlines and performance? It is important to reprioritize *being* and *doing* and begin to pray over it, seeking God's help and guidance to reclaim it and maintain it in every area of your life. Only then can you sow good seed in the lives of those you love.

The third statement is the conclusion that flows from the previous two, that *God is primarily concerned with the transformation of our hearts rather than the transaction of our business.* So let me ask you:

- *What does this process of transformation look like in your journey?*

- *In your life, what is most in need of being changed and transformed?*

- *When you think about God calling you on a journey from transaction and doing to transformation and being, where do you see Him working in that transformation?*

You can't lead others on that journey if you're not on that journey yourself. Herein lies one of the greatest hypocrisies in the Kingdom of God: people who are poor personal stewards trying to do development work in the name of Jesus. We have spiritually stagnant people in charge of a ministry of seed sowing. We have transactional people developing plans and strategies for a work of ministry that is wholly transformational.

So the question is how does all of this affect the way you conduct your fundraising work? How much differently would you look at the people from whom you solicit funds if your call as a Christian development person is to enter into their journey and be used by God to sow good seed into their lives? This good seed is God's instrument to help transform every one of our supporters into more godly stewards.

This insight was a paradigm shift for me. When I realized that my primary calling as a development person was to be used by God to cultivate hearts to be rich toward Him, everything I did changed. My prayer life changed. I no longer prayed, "Dear God, please help me be successful in raising money from Mr. and Mrs. Smith." My new prayer was, "Dear God, help me discern how You want to use me as an instrument in their journey to become more godly stewards." And I found that if I followed God's lead and allowed myself to be used by God for this purpose, spiritual growth happened in their lives *and* in mine. Through their changed hearts, God supplied all of our need according to His glorious riches!

God blesses the seed we sow. As people become more godly stewards, they give more freely, more joyfully and more sacrificially. But it is still a journey. The recent recession has provided us with an unprecedented window of opportunity. Seldom have we been given a greater opportunity to walk that path with our supporters. Many of them are deeply concerned, even scared. They have seen a decrease in the value of the assets God entrusted to them, and many have lost jobs or had significant reductions in work. They are asking questions. They are looking for people who care about them, and if we come alongside them and understand we are called to make that journey with them, we can minister in unprecedented ways.

For this and so many other reasons, it is critical that we understand the ministry nature of our job. The move from transaction to transformation is God's work, but we are His hands and feet. We are sowers, so our seed bags must be full.

Move from Two-Kingdom Bondage to One-Kingdom Freedom

"Where is our treasure?
Is it on earth, or in heaven?
What are we doing? What is the aim of our lives?
Are we just living to accumulate money,
or to get a position in the world for our children?
Or, are we trying to secure those treasures,
which we can safely lay up in heaven,
becoming rich toward God?"[2]

⇌ Dwight Lyman Moody ⇌

The second part of this journey is from the owner to the steward. More specifically, it is from two-kingdom bondage to one-Kingdom freedom. A brief overview of the theology of the godly steward helps to explain this second part of the journey.

We know we were created in the image of our triune God: Father, Son and Holy Spirit. The God we know through Jesus Christ is relational in His very nature, mutually indwelling and eternally in relationship with His Father and with the Holy Spirit. We were created in that image. As such, we are commanded and equipped to live in the image of a God Who, in His very nature, is relationship. That's the starting point for understanding the concept of the biblical steward.

When we read the Genesis account, we understand that God created us for relationships at four levels: our relationship with God, our relationship with our self, our relationship with our neighbor and our relationship with creation. Adam and Eve did not have to work or try to find themselves to figure out what life was all about. Adam and Eve walked with God in the cool of the evening—first level wholeness. We were also created for a whole relationship with our self, to have a full understanding of who we were, why we are here, and our true purpose in life. Adam and Eve were created to love God and tend the garden—second level wholeness. We were also created for whole relationship with our neighbor, to love our neighbor as we love our self. When we know and love ourselves, only then can we know and love our neighbor as we love ourselves— third level wholeness. Finally, we were created for whole relationships with the world that was brought into being by our Creator. We were put in a garden and given the command and privilege to tend the garden—fourth level wholeness. Genesis 1-2 paints a picture of the first man and woman in whole, healthy, and life-giving relationships at all four levels. That was God's purpose in creating us in His image.

Unfortunately, it didn't stay that way. We know that when sin entered the world, it brought brokenness at all four levels. Our relationship with God was broken. Banished from the garden, humanity could only approach God with fear and trembling, using mediators to stand before God and ask for forgiveness.

Our relationship with the self was also broken. Suddenly Adam and Eve found themselves in a hostile world, estranged from God and wondering what it meant for their self-meaning and purpose. We spend our lives trying to figure that out again on this side of the fall.

Our relationship with our neighbor was broken. The first story after the fall was Cain's killing of Abel, which begins the history of "man's inhumanity to man."

Finally, there was a changed, broken relationship with the created world. After the fall, we defined dominion as domination, rule over as abuse of and subdue as exploit. Our hoarding and over-consumption of the world's resources along with our own struggle with money and possessions are all indicators of our brokenness at this fourth level.

The good news is that in through Jesus Christ, those relationships were restored on all four levels. Christ came to restore our relationship with God (we have been brought near Him through the blood of Christ), with our self (our purpose in life has been re-established), with our neighbor (we are now once again called to love our neighbor as ourselves and to serve our neighbor as unto Christ), and with the created world (we have been restored as stewards in Christ of God's precious creation; we are called again to take care of this wonderful world that God gave us).

On all four levels, these relationships were given to us in creation, lost in the fall, and fully redeemed by the blood of Christ. This means that each one has now been given back to us as a precious gift and we are *stewards* of these redeemed relationships on all four levels. So the definition of stewardship is *"reflecting our creator God through whole, redeemed relationships on all four levels, and glorifying God by practicing in each the ongoing work of the steward."*

This is a rich, theologically-sound, biblical understanding of what it means to be a steward in the Kingdom of God. The key to this definition is that we serve as stewards, not owners, of these relationships. They are not ours. They belong to the God who brought them back to us when we had lost them through our disobedience. We are commanded to nurture and honor and deepen these relationships. To do so, we must continually place them all into the hands of God and under His authority. When we do so, we live as one-Kingdom stewards. In this Kingdom there is only one Lord. Everything belongs to Him. Everything! Our relationships with God, ourselves, our neighbor, and creation have all been given back to us through Christ. It is all part of the Kingdom of God. Everything is subservient to one Lord in one Kingdom as one-Kingdom people. And we respond to this Lordship by serving as the godly steward.

The result of living as a one-Kingdom steward is freedom. If everything in your entire life is put under the one Kingdom of God, and if He is the Lord of everything in all four relationships, then you are freed to be a steward of those things. You don't have to own them.

You don't have to control them. You only have to take this wonderful gift that God has given and be a good steward of what you have. That is freedom!

On the other hand, as soon as we start to shift from stewards to owners, we will begin to experience bondage. It usually starts in the contours of our lives and in convenient places that pull us back into some foolish sense of ownership. Most often it starts with our stuff. This stuff can be possessions, but it can also be less tangible, like time. Some of us say that God can have everything He wants, as long as He lets us have control over how we spend our time. We all have areas of life over which we keep control and play the owner. "Play" is all it ever really can be. God is the ultimate Owner, and we can never be more than stewards, but with all of our grasping and clinging, we can be stewards in bondage. When we believe in our hearts that we truly own and control any aspect of our lives, we begin immediately to slide into bondage. It's an amazing thing. Think about it in your own life. The more money you have, the more anxious you become about it. The more things you possess, the more time you spend insuring them, fixing them, keeping them secure and worrying about them.

Playing the owner eats into your soul. The more you own a relation-ship with someone, the more that relationship is going to tear you apart. It is bondage. And the enemy knows it. That's why he said to Adam and Eve in the garden, "Did God really say you can't eat of any of these fruits...?" The first sin was an act of grasping at ownership, the ability to know right and wrong and judge for ourselves. Adam and Eve rejected the role of steward in favor of a chance to play God. The enemy deceived Adam and Eve in this way and is deceiving people the same way today. "Did God really say you had to give *everything* to Him? Come on, how about your leisure time? You're going on vacation, that's really *yours*, isn't it?"

As we buy the lie, we begin to build our own kingdom made up of stuff we seek to own and control. And every kingdom needs a king. If Christ is not the Lord, then who is the king? We decide that we are.

And so we divide up life into these two kingdoms; the kingdom of those things we are willing to let God have control over, and the kingdom of stuff we try to control ourselves.

Your job might be one of those things in your kingdom. If you believe that you absolutely must have your job, that you cannot afford to lose your job, that you don't know what you would do if you ever lost your job, then you are playing the owner of that job. As you try to control it, it will put you in bondage. If you want to be free, then say to God, "Lord, you have me here for a time, when you are finished, move me on. I know you will prepare another place for me. In the meantime, I will live in freedom in my relationship with my job."

When we move from stewards to owners, we go from being the servant of the Lord to being lord over servants. And we sacrifice freedom for this counterfeit idea of control. Let's compare two stories side-by-side to illustrate this point. The first is from Matthew 19:16-22.

> Now a man came to Jesus and asked, "Teacher, what good thing must I do to get eternal life?" "Why do you ask me what is good?" Jesus replied, "There is only one who is good. If you want to enter life, obey the commandments." "Which ones?" the man inquired. Jesus replied "Do not murder. Do not commit adultery, do not steal, do not give false testimony, honor your father and mother and love your neighbor as yourself." "These I have kept," the young man said, "What do I still lack?" Jesus answered, "If you want to be perfect, go, sell your possessions and give to the poor, and you will have treasure in heaven. Then come, follow me." When the young man heard this, he went away sad, because he had great wealth.

Look at the passage in this way: this young man asked a two-kingdom question and Jesus gave a one-Kingdom response. The man said, in essence, "I still want to live in my two kingdoms, I still want to have my wealth over here but also to fulfill the requirements of the law, so given this two-kingdom mindset, what do I have to do to inherit eternal life?" And Jesus said, "It is simple: just have one Kingdom. Give it all away and follow me." And we are told the young ruler went away sad, because he could not step off the throne of his own kingdom.

Now look at Matthew 13:44. Jesus is speaking:

> The kingdom of heaven is like a treasure hidden in a field. When a man found it, he hid it again and then in his joy he went and sold all that he had and bought that field.

What a contrast! The young ruler had so much but could not give it to Christ, so he went away sad. The other man was so excited in finding the Kingdom of God that he gladly sold everything he had in the world in order to buy the great treasure hidden in a field. That is one-Kingdom living.

In John 8:31-36, Jesus speaks powerfully on this freedom, "I came so that you might have freedom, to free you from bondage and from sin, and if the Son sets you free, you will be free indeed."

Our prayer for every one of you is that you know freedom as a child of God, and that you can help your supporters know that same freedom. If God can use you to help your supporters on their journey to freedom as one-Kingdom disciples, then you have served the Kingdom of God in an incredible way. It may not show up on a pie chart in a board report, but it shows up in the Kingdom of heaven, and God will bless it.

Take a look at your development work, your fundraising techniques, your annual fund plans, your major gifts strategy and everything else you do in your profession, and ask the question, "Where is it reflected that I am helping our supporters become one-Kingdom people to be freed for joyous response?" We challenge you to give that presentation to your board. Tell them you believe this is your calling, and as a result you believe that God is going to bless your work, and in turn, your ministry will have the funds it needs to carry out its mission.

That board report may be years away, but until then, we plant seeds. We are sowers of understanding in the lives of our organizations. We are sowers of right practices based on biblical truth. And we are sowers of one-Kingdom living in the lives of our co-workers, our givers, our family and our church. Your job is to sow seeds that set people free! How cool is that!

It all begins with a look in the mirror. What is God doing in your life to free you from the bondage of two-kingdom living? Ask yourself that every day. Pray for God to show you where you are in bondage to a two-kingdom lifestyle and pray to be set free. If you are a development officer, you need mentors and colleagues to walk with you. Get to know others in this field. Find a mentoring relationship, talk to one another, and pray together. We are all on the journey to freedom.

Focus on Cultivating Hearts that Will Joyously Become Stewards

*"Used properly, money can facilitate some great experiences.
Used improperly, it can be devastating.
But the fact is that true joy and happiness
are there for the taking
no matter whether you have much money or little.
The proper alignment of God's purpose in your life
with your relationships and resources
brings ultimate fulfillment."*[3]

⇒ *Alan Gotthardt* ⇐

The idea of our free response contradicts a tendency we have in the Christian faith to make the good news of the gospel sound more like a contract. Some of our language and teaching sounds like this:

Jesus did his part—died on the cross and rose again–and so God's part of the contract has been fulfilled. Now it is up to us to fulfill our obligation. Being a Christian means adding our work to God's work to complete the contract. We are called to repent, say the right prayers, go to church, change our lives and live for Jesus; all as an obligation to our part of the agreement.

So we live a Christian life in a contractual way as if we owe God debts of behavior we need to pay to fulfill our part of the divine agreement. How many of us have grown up under this teaching?

There is another response, the free and joyous response of the child of God. To illustrate the difference, imagine we have two manila envelopes each containing $10,000. We approach two people, Greg and Donna. To Greg we say "Greg, here's the deal. You can have the cash in this envelope, but here's what you have to do. When we give this to you, at precisely the moment that you get it, stand up, turn around, put your hands in the air and yell 'Hallelujah!' Now, you must stand up at exactly the right time, turn around in the right way, shout in the right tone and key and loud enough so that everybody can hear you. If you do it exactly as we told you, then you can keep the money." We then take the other manila envelope and hand it to Donna and say, "Donna, here's $10,000; it's yours, no strings attached. Enjoy it."

Consider what happens next. Greg stands up and, at exactly the right moment, turns around just as instructed, puts his hands in the air, yells "Hallelujah!" just the way he was instructed. And what does Donna do? She stands up, turns around, throws her hands in the air and yells, "Hallelujah!" Both gave the same response but had totally different motivations. Greg was fulfilling an obligation in order to achieve a reward. Donna was so overwhelmed by an undeserved and extravagant gift that all she could do was respond in gratitude and joy. We think Jesus wants us to live our lives like Donna. When we learn of what Christ has done for us, we respond by jumping up in the air and yelling "Hallelujah!" That is a response of freedom and joy.

Listen to Paul exhort the Corinthians (2 Corinthians 8:1-9) to just such a free and joyous response:

> Now, and now my brothers and sisters, we want you to know about the grace that God has given the Macedonian churches. Out of the most severe trial, their overflowing joy and their extreme poverty, welled up in rich generosity. For I testify that they gave as much as they were able and even beyond their ability. Entirely on their own, they urgently pleaded with us for the privilege of sharing in this service with the saints. And they did not do as we expected, but they gave themselves first to the Lord, and then to us in keeping with God's will. So we urge Titus, since he had earlier made a beginning, to bring also to completion this act of grace on your part. But just as you excel

in everything, in faith, in speech, in knowledge, in complete earnestness and in your love for us, see that you also excel in this grace of giving.

Did you hear the call to joyous response of the Macedonians? Giving themselves first to the Lord; sharing beyond what was asked of them; their overwhelming joy, welling up inside of them, moved them to participate in this collection.

Part of our journey is cultivating hearts that will make a free and joyous response to our call to be godly stewards, rather than a sense of legal obligation. It requires us to sow good seed into the lives of our supporters. And it begins with us. Again, we cannot sow what we do not have. Our seed bags must be full. So which type of response best typifies your own attitude of giving? Are you a joyful giver? Do you give out of the deep gratitude and joy of your heart? Can you hardly wait to respond to what God has done in your life?

And then, in your fundraising practices, which of the two are you encouraging? Do we use guilt or obligation or promises of blessing for generosity or other contractual incentives to give? Or do we proclaim God's incredible grace and abundance and encourage our people to respond as Jesus invites us to respond when he said, "God loves a cheerful giver, who gives out of the joy of their heart"?

How would your work be affected if you believed that God uses your vocation, your calling, to help your supporters in their journey to becoming more godly stewards? How would your daily work be affected if your single goal was to help your supporters know the joy of their free response of generous giving to God's work?

Grow as a Sower

"How are all things sanctified to us,
but in the separation and dedication of them to God?
Are they not all his talents,
and must be employed in his service?
Must not every Christian first ask,
In what way may I most honour God with my substance?" [4]

☞ *Richard Baxter (1615-1691)* ☜

If you are responsible for raising resources for God's work, you are a sower. Your seed is your work of cultivating hearts to be rich toward God. And your seed bag is full only to the extent that you start with your own heart first. If you are free as a one-Kingdom steward and your life is a joyous response to the grace of God, you can undertake your development work in a way that sets people free for their own response of joy. This work is intensely personal; it starts with us, and then it allows us to be instruments in God's hands to bring about transformation in the lives of the people to whom we minister.

Here are five spiritual disciplines to practice as you continue on your journey to becoming a sower in God's Kingdom.

1. **Start each morning with a conscious commitment to go through your day with the mindset of a sower.**

   - Pray that people come into your life who need good seed sown in their lives.

   - Pray for discernment to see them, hear them, recognize them, and to have the capacity to sow into their lives exactly what they need.

   - End each day with a prayer of thanks as you name the people into whose lives you were able to sow good seed.

25

2. **Start each morning by opening yourself up to God's correcting Spirit to help you see in yourself the places where you most need to grow as a godly steward.**

- Pray for openness to see your own Kingdom-building attitudes.

- Ask for forgiveness where you have played the lord over your own kingdom.

- Re-submit everything you have and everything you are to Christ and His absolute Lordship of your life.

3. **Start each morning asking God to fill your seed bag.**

- Pray for godly wisdom in every decision you make.

- Pray for discernment that you may hear God's voice and know His leading as you walk through your day.

- Pray for a deep sense of God's love and grace that you might truly be God's worker sowing life, hope, and joy in the lives of your colleagues, co-workers, supporters, friends and family.

4. **At work, start each day praying with your team (or trusted colleagues).**

- Pray fervently for your supporters and partners, that God would use you and your organization to help develop hearts that are rich toward God.

- Pray for pure motives and right attitudes as you plan for and interact with every supporter.

- Pray for opportunities to share your ministry and its goals with people who have a similar passion.

- Pray in faith for God's abundant blessings on your work.

5. Celebrate and rejoice over every act of giving.

- Ask God to help you cultivate a heart that searches for the support of God's work through the generous and joyous response of God's people.

- Celebrate it wherever and whenever you see it.

- Strive for a culture of joy and celebration in your development work as you see God "bring the increase" into your daily work of sowing.

One plants, another waters, but God—and God alone—brings the increase. May we dedicate our lives to sowing good seeds into the lives of everyone around us, and trust God to bless that work a hundred-fold. To God be the glory!

PART II

The Seasons of Work
for the Sower

Gary G. Hoag

Now that you have a biblical context for raising resources, for helping you understand your calling as a sower, this next part aims at providing practical application, so you can touch the lives of others by applying these truths to your life and work.

If, in reading so far, you have moved from two-kingdom bondage to one-Kingdom freedom, this section will show you how to set others free. Whether you are a CEO, a Christian leader, or simply a faithful steward, if you want to unleash radical levels of giving rooted in gratitude, then read on for guidance in helping others grow in the grace of giving.

Ultimately, this is a spiritual and strategic manual for raising more than money. Rather it redefines raising Kingdom resources as raising up stewards to be rich toward God.

The idea of being a steward who is *rich toward God* comes from Luke 12:13-21.

> Someone in the crowd said to him, "Teacher, tell my brother to divide the inheritance with me."
>
> Jesus replied, "Man, who appointed me a judge or an arbiter between you?" Then he said to them, "Watch out! Be on your guard against all kinds of greed; a man's life does not consist in the abundance of his possessions."
>
> And he told them this parable: "The ground of a certain rich man produced a good crop. He thought to himself, 'What shall I do? I have no place to store my crops.'
>
> Then he said, 'This is what I'll do. I will tear down my barns and build bigger ones, and there I will store all my grain and my goods. And I'll say to myself, 'You have plenty of good things laid up for many years. Take life easy; eat, drink and be merry.'

But God said to him, 'You fool! This very night your life will be demanded from you. Then who will get what you have prepared for yourself?'

This is how it will be with anyone who stores up things for himself but is not rich toward God."

Jesus wanted people to understand that storing up treasures on earth is the opposite of being *rich toward God*. So what should people do when they have a bountiful harvest? What should people do with their treasures? Jesus answers that question in Matthew 6:19-21.

Do not store up for yourselves treasures on earth, where moth and rust destroy, and where thieves break in and steal. But store up for yourselves treasures in heaven, where moth and rust do not destroy, and where thieves do not break in and steal. For where your treasure is, there your heart will be also.

Jesus wants people to store up their treasures in heaven through generous giving for Kingdom purposes—starting with local church support and extending to ministries in your region and around the world. This will accomplish the *Great Commission*, sharing the Gospel of eternal salvation, and you will also fulfill the *Great Commandment* to love the Lord your God with all your heart, soul, mind and strength (which includes all your resources) and love your neighbor as yourself. Thus your giving spans from the local church to a host of regional and national ministries to serving the poor anywhere in the world.

Paul echoes the teachings of Jesus in First Timothy 6:17-19. Paul outlines for Timothy a message for the rich Christians of Ephesus.

Command those who are rich in this present world not to be arrogant nor to put their hope in wealth, which is so uncertain, but to put their hope in God, who richly provides us with everything for our enjoyment. Command them to do good, to be rich in good deeds, and to be generous and willing to share. In this way they will lay up treasure for themselves as a firm foundation for the coming age, so that they may take hold of the life that is truly life.

Paul wanted Timothy to tell the wealthy to become regular givers who openhandedly let go of possessions. These stewards will store up treasure for the future and right now grasp the life that is truly life. Rather than relying on uncertain wealth, which tempts its possessor to trust in it, the giver takes hold of God as the only certain foundation for life, thereby advancing God's Kingdom purposes.

Since the calling of the sower is to be a steward rich toward God, the work of the sower is to raise up such stewards. Instead of seeking gifts for the ministries they serve, the sower helps those with financial wealth become givers who grasp these biblical truths. Let us look at this practical advice in the form of an almanac.

An almanac is an agricultural publication based on the calendar and sowing seasons. It contains facts about the ordered universe and collective wisdom from generations of farmers to help others be as fruitful as possible.

If you pick up any farmer's almanac, you will notice two characteristics. First, the *precise understanding* of the ordered universe is mind-boggling. For any day in the year, the almanac can tell you exactly what time the sun will rise and set. It can sketch the position of the stars in the sky. It can tell you about the status of the tides or the moon in its cycle. The almanac also contains seasonal advice in the form of answers to real questions. In winter, what should a farmer do to prepare the soil for sowing and when? When in the spring should a farmer sow seed? What must a farmer do to cultivate and irrigate the crop based on projected summer rainfall for the region? When should the farmer reap the harvest? The almanac helps prevent a farmer from making costly mistakes.

There are also specific formulae omitted in an almanac. Nowhere is there a set of steps that guarantees success for sowers. Why? Farmers lean on the wisdom of generations and their own experience, and then get to work, trusting God to bring the increase. There's no magic formula that guarantees results.

In adapting the format of the almanac to the ministry of raising Kingdom resources, the sower—or farmer—is the Christian reading this book and the seed is the biblical stewardship principles found in God's Word. God, of course, is the One who makes the seed grow, the One who works in the hearts of givers to help them become more generous; the fields are the lives we touch; and the seasonal advice is the collective wisdom from past sowers who understand how to effectively raise Kingdom resources.

The Seasons of Work for Sowers

Let's now focus on the *seasons of work* to help sowers be as fruitful as possible—without promising results that only God can deliver. This collective wisdom from experienced sowers will be presented in four sections for the four seasons: winter, spring, summer, and fall. And even as there are twelve months in the year, each season will offer three sections of advice (see Appendix A — Almanac Summary at a Glance, pages 77-78).

Winter is a time of preparation: both sower and soil must be prepared before broadcasting seed. In this season, we will take a fresh look at the role of the sower, how to fill seed bags and what to do to prepare soil. In resource development language, the leader's winter work is understanding the role of a steward-raiser rather than merely a fundraiser.

Spring is the season for sowing biblical principles. To sow spiritual seed takes skill; it also requires faith that God will cause life to burst forth. Sowers face hindrances that stunt the growth of stewards and they must understand these pitfalls to have productive planting.

Summer is the season for spiritual growth. Specific guidance in this section helps you understand where people are in the stewardship journey so you can nurture their growth. Spiritual work not only requires specific attention to what is taking place in the fields, it also calls for a community of workers. A sower may cast countless seeds in various fields, but nurturing many souls requires assistance. This section outlines practical ideas for rallying laborers to work with you in the ministry of encouraging Christian generosity.

Fall is harvest time. For this season, we offer insights for reaping in a way to make the harvest most fruitful, including size of the crop, trends in harvesting, and celebrating with thanksgiving. An almanac will tell you that not all harvests are directly tied to the work and care of the sowers; sometimes seasons of abundance prevail or crops fail. The focus will be how sowers can maximize abundance in the fields where God has placed them, regardless of the circumstances. In practical ministry terms, this section demonstrates that you reap what you sow. If you sow biblical stewardship principles in people's lives, they will become more generous.

Any preparation for sowing spiritual seed must start with the message from the parable of the soils found in Mark 4:1-8. Consider the words of Jesus in this parable as the preface to the almanac.

> Again Jesus began to teach by the lake. The crowd that gathered around him was so large that he got into a boat and sat in it out on the lake, while all the people were along the shore at the water's edge. He taught them many things by parables, and in his teaching said: "Listen! A farmer went

out to sow his seed. As he was scattering the seed, some fell
along the path, and the birds came and ate it up. Some fell on
rocky places, where it did not have much soil. It sprang up
quickly, because the soil was shallow. But when the sun came
up, the plants were scorched, and they withered because they
had no root. Other seed fell among thorns, which grew up
and choked the plants, so that they did not bear grain. Still
other seed fell on good soil. It came up, grew and produced
a crop, multiplying thirty, sixty, or even a hundred times."

Then Mark records Jesus' explanation of this parable in verses 14 – 20.

The farmer sows the word. Some people are like seed along
the path, where the word is sown. As soon as they hear it,
Satan comes and takes away the word that was sown in them.
Others, like seed sown on rocky places, hear the word and at
once receive it with joy. But since they have no root, they last
only a short time. When trouble or persecution comes
because of the word, they quickly fall away. Still others, like
seed sown among thorns, hear the word; but the worries of
this life, the deceitfulness of wealth and the desires for other
things come in and choke the word, making it unfruitful.
Others, like seed sown on good soil, hear the word, accept it,
and produce a crop—thirty, sixty or even a hundred times
what was sown.

This parable teaches us many spiritual lessons as we prepare to
look at the work of the sower. The seed is the same for everyone:
it is the Word of God. The sower's role is to sow seed everywhere.
In different environments, factors help or hinder the fruitfulness
of the seed; fertile soil welcomes seed, while birds, rocks and
weeds limit or prevent growth. Different soils produce harvests
of varying sizes. Some plants wither and die. Others sprout, but
produce no fruit, and some produce a crop thirty-, sixty-, and
one-hundredfold.

The conclusion of this parable—the size of the harvest—may be the most important lesson of all to inspire you to become a sower. If a good harvest is either more than or equal to a thirtyfold harvest, Jesus' parable gives not just good news but the greatest news ever told: sow the Word of God in the lives of people and it can produce a good harvest, double a good harvest, or a harvest beyond imagination.

In the spirit of this parable, let us fill our seed bags with stewardship principles from the Word of God, sow abundantly, knowing that some seed will produce no fruit in the hearts of those who receive it, some will produce a good harvest, some a great harvest, and in a few, an unimaginable harvest will be reaped. Thus we will redefine the work of fundraising as "the transformational ministry of raising Kingdom resources."

The Season of Preparation — Winter

*"It is natural to feel fear and insecurity when confronted with
the radical demands of the Christian commitment.
But enveloped in the lived truths of God's furious love,
insecurity is swallowed up in the solidity of agape,
and anguish and fear give way to hope and desire.
The Christian becomes aware that God's appeal for
unlimited generosity from His people has been preceded
from His side by a limitless love, a love so intent
upon a response that He has empowered us to respond
through the gift of His own Holy Spirit."* [5]

⌖ *Brennan Manning* ⌖

God's call for each of us to live a life of unlimited generosity is
rooted in His limitless love and care for us and in His provision
of the Holy Spirit to empower us! Every sower must grasp this in
winter before helping others understand it in the spring and
summer. Winter is the season of preparation, both for you, the
sower, and your audience, the soil. There are three actions of
seasonal advice in winter: understand your role as a sower, fill your
seed bags, and till the fields for sowing.

Seasonal Overview: The Work of the Sower in Winter	
Secular Fundraising	**Biblical Steward-raising**
1. Leaders consider their role as being the *fundraisers* for the organization.	1. Leaders understand their role is to sow biblical stewardship principles; God is *the Fundraiser*.
2. Leaders strategize to get people to make gifts to their organizations.	2. Leaders gather biblical truths that encourage people to become givers who are rich toward God.
3. Leaders do whatever works to get people to respond generously.	3. Leaders model generosity and pray for God to help people grow spiritually in the grace of giving.
Figure 1. The first season: preparation.	

1. Understand Your Role as a Sower

Whatever your position, as a follower of Jesus your primary role is to sow seed. That job is to sow, not to sow *and* make things grow. We fall into the trap of believing we can make our constituents give sacrificially, that we can convince our congregation to be more generous, or that we cause our children to become givers. The truth is that all these outcomes are out of our control and rest solely in God's hands. So what is our role? Our job is to sow seed in the hearts of people and trust God to take care of making it grow in their lives.

In the secular world as well as the Christian community, people assume it is the leader's job to be the fundraiser. So if you are a leader, and you broach the topic of giving, get the conversation off on the right foot by making this point very clear. Articulate that God is the Fundraiser; He is the One Who works in people's hearts to move them to participate in His work through giving. If you don't, they will think you see yourself as a fundraiser. In addition, boldly communicate that your role is to raise up givers for God's Kingdom through sowing biblical stewardship principles in people's lives.

By taking this approach, you leave the fundraising results up to God; the pressure is off you and the giver. Your interaction helps others grow in the grace of giving because you demonstrate you care more about their spiritual condition than whether or not they make a gift to your ministry. Your role is to urge them to chart a course of being rich toward God. Furthermore, you are encouraging their giving to go to whatever ministries God leads them to support, not just to the ministry you serve. You are there to encourage stewards to be involved in the King's business.

Jeavons and Basinger echo this perspective in *Growing Givers Hearts: Treating Fundraising as Ministry.* They state that the ultimate role of the Christian leader is to "make the process of fundraising one that nurtures and facilitates growth in faith for the donors." [6]

Consider the following true story. When a candidate interviewed for a chief development officer position at a Christian organization, the president informed him that his primary responsibility would be to raise $1.2 million each year for the annual operating fund. Cordially, the candidate responded that he could not take the job with that understanding since he saw God's role as the Fundraiser and his role as encouraging people to participate in God's work in many ways, one of which would be through their giving.

The president mentioned the past successful fundraising highlights from his resume. The candidate rejoined that those results came through faithfully sharing with people what God was doing and challenging them to participate through their prayers, gifts and volunteer service. The president looked relieved, at last understanding what was and was not the primary responsibility of the chief development officer. This freed him to rethink his own role in inviting people to participate in the ministry's work, and how he would manage this new staff member. From that point forward, both were free to get at the real job—raising up givers who want to be generously involved with God in His work.

Before encouraging generous giving, the Christian leader, pastor and parent must understand their roles in the process, which is not to make things grow but rather to sow bountifully. To help stewards become rich toward God, you must do more than share the ministry's financial needs; you must provide a reason for their involvement. You must sow these concepts in their hearts.

At this moment, take an inventory of your own life. If you are called to help people grow as a steward, be assured that God will want you to grow more deeply in this area as well. If you are not interested in taking such a spiritual journey, please consider a different role than that of a Christian leader, stewardship officer or pastor. Why? In that role, you are in a position to have an incalculable impact for the Kingdom, so if you are not interested in sowing, please hand the bag of seed to someone else.

If you want to proceed, but still struggle with thinking that it is your job to secure transactions, flip back to the first part of this book and read the sections you underlined; your pen may well have been guided by the Holy Spirit. In winter you must remember what your role is and isn't, and embrace it; you will find yourself walking in one-Kingdom freedom.

Summary: The role of the sower is to sow as much seed as possible and trust God to make it grow.

2. Fill Your Seed Bags

To sow abundantly you need lots of seed. To sow biblical stewardship principles in your life, in the lives of your children, in the people who attend your church, or in the hearts of those who partner with you, you must gather as much seed as possible. You cannot share with others what you yourself have not taken the time to grasp.

The seed represents stewardship principles found in limitless supply in the Word of God.[7] A new resource highlighting these principles is the *NIV Stewardship Study Bible* published by Zondervan.[8] It contains an index of thousands of verses related to the handling of money and possessions, profiles of faithful stewards, stewardship challenges and reading plans for meditation and contemplation. This is the first-ever resource of its kind to highlight stewardship principles from Genesis to Revelation. In it you will read through God's Word anew. Have your seed bag close by, and make a list of verses to share with those you serve. Performing this exercise will transform you and prepare you to serve as an agent of transformation.

Henri J. M. Nouwen explains that such transformational process is necessary before anyone can talk about money. "Those of us who ask for money need to look carefully at ourselves. The question is not how to get money. Rather the question is about our relationship with money. We will never be able to ask for money if we do not know how we ourselves relate to money."[9]

Some students in my seminary course, Stewardship and Resource Development, said they wanted to learn how to preach about money or to raise money for their ministries. From the beginning, though, the focus of the class is to walk students through the Scriptures so the biblical stewardship principles will transform their understanding of life as stewards in His Kingdom.

Sometime during the course, most students testify to experiencing the conversion Luther described as the conversion of the purse: the shift from being a servant of money to being a servant of God.

Are you a servant of money, a.k.a. Mammon, or are you a servant of God? How can you tell? If you would not be willing to let go of everything you have to follow God, then you are a slave to Mammon.

As was mentioned earlier in this book, consider the case of the rich young ruler in Luke 18:18-23. Jesus encouraged him to exchange his worldly wares for heavenly treasures. Rather than owning his possessions, his possessions clearly owned him.

> A certain ruler asked him, "Good teacher, what must I do to inherit eternal life?" "Why do you call me good?" Jesus answered. "No one is good—except God alone. You know the commandments: 'Do not commit adultery, do not murder, do not steal, do not give false testimony, honor your father and mother.'" "All these I have kept since I was a boy," he said. When Jesus heard this, he said to him, "You still lack one thing. Sell everything you have and give to the poor, and you will have treasure in heaven. Then come, follow me." When he heard this, he became very sad, because he was a man of great wealth.

On the other hand, some of the first disciples, fishermen, demonstrated their willingness to let go of everything as they left their nets when invited to follow Jesus in Matthew 4:18-22.

> As Jesus was walking beside the Sea of Galilee, he saw two brothers, Simon called Peter and his brother Andrew. They were casting a net into the lake, for they were fishermen. "Come, follow me," Jesus said, "and I will make you fishers of men." At once they left their nets and followed him. Going on from there, he saw two other brothers, James son of Zebedee and his brother John. They were in a boat with their father Zebedee, preparing their nets. Jesus called them, and immediately they left the boat and their father and followed him.

Do you need to leave something behind to follow Jesus?

Nouwen echoes this perspective, saying, "If our security is totally in God, then we are free to ask for money. Only when we are free from money can we ask freely for others to give it."[10] The only way to become free from serving money is to let go of it in order to grasp God. Then you are in a position to freely serve God and call others to use money as God has outlined.

In winter, your work is to immerse yourself in biblical principles that remind you of God's infinite provision for His people, from providing manna in the wilderness of the Old Testament to calling us to depend on Him for our daily bread in the Lord's Prayer of the New Testament. You must be completely immersed in these concepts so they drip from your tongue later.

Summary: To be a sower of biblical principles, you must fill your seed bag. The only place to find seed is in the Bible; therein can be found endless supply of seed for sowing abundantly.

3. Prepare Yourself for Planting

Your seed bags are full, and you understand your role. Now what? Every farmer knows that before you can sow, the soil must be tilled, and this is hard work. Digging furrows demands toil and sweat. Softening hard ground means multiple passes with the plow. Generally the window of time when the ground can be worked is short, so you must map out a plan to get the fields ready.

As a sower of spiritual seed, you must intentionally identify where to plant stewardship principles. Where to plant is the part you can control. So how do you prepare the soil? Share the word, model Christian generosity, and pray for others to follow.

Modeling Christian generosity is a way of life, described here by Lauren Tyler Wright as a lifelong journey.

> We cannot simply "achieve" a lifestyle of generosity, reap the benefits and check it off our list. Rather, we learn the practice of generosity while we walk our faith journey, step by step, finding joy and fulfillment in each segment, and always seeking to grow through various spiritual practices. This is great news because it means we do not have to "master" the practice before we experience its rewards.[11]

The most profound way to invite others to follow is to walk down the path first, and you can start today. On that note, Wright adds this thought:

> While the goal is to create a lifestyle, you have to start some-where. Don't be afraid to start small. It's the intentionality and regularity of the act that is most important, not the size of the gift. Think of it as a mosaic of small practices that, before you know it, add up to a lifestyle.[12]

Live and give generously if you want others to follow. People will hear you because they see it modeled in your life.

The other thing you can do to prepare the soils to receive the truth is to pray for them. Pray specifically, asking God to do what you cannot do, to soften the hard ground of people's hearts. Ask God to open their eyes to see His abundance in a world of seemingly scarce resources. Ask God to open their ears to hear that He knows more about their needs than they do and desires their trust in His provision when most people seek to secure their own future. Ask God to help people avoid storing up treasures susceptible to market corrections, but rather exchange them for heavenly treasures that will never decline in value. Pray that people will be willing to think differently about money than how the world has shaped them to think.

Before you can sow, you must understand your role, fill your seed bag, and prepare the soil by modeling Christian generosity and praying for others to follow your example. Do that, and you will be prepared for spring, the season of sowing.

Summary: *Model Christian generosity and pray that God will help people grasp life-changing stewardship principles.*

The Season for Sowing Seed — Spring

"God's ownership of everything
also changes the kind of question we ask in giving.
Rather than 'How much of my money should I give to God?'
we learn to ask 'How much of God's money
should I keep for myself?'
The difference between these two questions
is of monumental proportions."[13]

Richard Foster

Biblical principles change everything—the questions we ask, how we approach life. And when it comes to money, they change our values by literally turning them right side up! Transformational thinking goes far beyond money, too, when we realize stewardship extends to the use of our spiritual gifts, abilities and everything else under our management. As you grow in this aspect, you will want your family, church and ministry members to grow too! The best way to help them grow is to plant stewardship principles in their lives.

The spring section of this spiritual almanac shows how to map out a plan for planting this kind of seed in people's lives. It also outlines dangers you face in the field as well as tips for encouraging growth in seedlings.

Seasonal Overview: The Work of the Sower in Spring	
Secular Fundraising	**Biblical Steward-raising**
4. Leaders seek transactions: gifts to accomplish their organizations' purposes from donors who have financial resources.	4. Leaders seek transformation: to help others use the spiritual and material gifts entrusted to them to accomplish God's work.
5. Leaders reinforce worldly thinking through strategies such as public donor recognition that may work culturally but be inconsistent biblically.	5. Leaders help people discern between worldly thinking and godly thinking by modeling biblical stewardship principles.
6. "It's all about relationships!" The leader's goal is to build relationships with people that will result in many gifts over many years.	6. "It's all about the most important relationship!" The leader's goal is to draw people closer to God. As a result they will be more generously involved in God's work.

Figure 2. The second season: broadcasting seed.

4. Planting the Seed in Yourselves First

If you serve as a ministry leader, you know your role is to discern God's vision for the ministry you serve and trust Him to provide to accomplish that vision. This only happens through faith, yet you have a clear-cut job to do. You invite stewards to join you in doing whatever work God has set forth. Their participation is to be more than financial; it is also through prayer and personal involvement.

This point is illustrated well in the tabernacle campaign in Exodus 25-36. In Exodus 25:1-2 the text clearly outlines the job Moses is to undertake. "The LORD said to Moses, 'Tell the Israelites to bring me an offering. You are to receive the offering for me from each man whose heart prompts him to give.'" So Moses was told to ask the people for an offering and receive what God moved people to give willingly.

Moses was not only told to ask people to make financial contributions, he was also to urge them to use their abilities to accomplish the work, as Exodus 28:3 recounts. "Tell all the skilled men to whom I have given wisdom in such matters, that they are to make garments for Aaron, for his consecration, so he may serve me as priest."

During the campaign effort, people forgot God's ways and were disciplined, and soon thereafter, an intimate conversation between God and Moses provides insights to encourage generosity for leaders today. Exodus 33:15-16 states: "Then Moses said to him, 'If your presence does not go with us, do not send us up from here. How will anyone know that you are pleased with me and with your people unless you go with us? What else will distinguish me and your people from all the other people on the face of the earth?'"

Moses is crying out, asking God to guide the efforts He had called His people to do. Every leader should mirror Moses' attitude through interceding and inviting others to intercede, to serve as a light to the world, different from those who follow the ways of the world.

Of course the tabernacle campaign story ends with people being moved in their hearts to give more than enough to finish the project—not by the leader, but by God. As Exodus 36:2-5 proclaims:

> Then Moses summoned Bezalel and Oholiab and every skilled person to whom the Lord had given ability and who was willing to come and do the work. They received from Moses all the offerings the Israelites had brought to carry out the work of constructing the sanctuary. And the people continued to bring freewill offerings morning after morning. So all the skilled craftsmen who were doing all the work on the sanctuary left their work and said to Moses, "The people are

bringing more than enough for doing the work the Lord commanded to be done."

This story illustrates four parts that should comprise the plan of the leader who wants to plant stewardship principles. Your efforts must invite people to participate in more than just giving. As a leader, consider this purpose statement:

The purpose of our stewardship efforts is to ask constituents and new friends to participate with God in His work at _____ through offering (1) *involvement* opportunities and (2) *instruction* in biblical stewardship while encouraging (3) *intercession* and (4) *investment* in the ministry.

This statement captures the theme of Exodus 25-36 and is summarized by *four I's*: (1) involvement, (2) instruction, (3) intercession and (4) investment.[14] Besides giving, or *investment*, encourage *involvement* through service based on people's skills and their *intercession* in prayer on behalf of the ministry while providing stewardship *instruction* to motivate people to participate in far greater ways.

When you plant the stewardship seeds of inviting people to serve using their God-given gifts, generous service sprouts. When you plant seeds urging people to intercede on behalf of the Lord's work, what sprouts is a community knit together witnessing God answering prayer. When you plant seeds by asking people to give from what God has given them, what sprouts is more than enough giving to accomplish the work. And when you plant seeds that instruct people in true stewardship, what sprouts is generosity that comes from a transformed life.

Spring is the time for planting seed. The secular world says "adopt whatever tactics you can to get people to make gifts." The work of the sower is different; sow biblical principles and you unleash holistic giving that will yield more than enough, just like the Exodus account.

Summary: Sowers sow seed that helps people do more than make gifts; it helps them become generous givers of all they are and all they have.

5. Dangers during the Sowing Season

In this section, we highlight the spiritual and social forces that endanger the planting of stewardship principles. If you recall the parable of the sower and the soils, outside forces can hinder the planting process from being successful, like the birds that ate the seed. Along the same line, circumstances can stop the sowing process from taking place; riches, the cares of the world, tribulation, and persecution all stop the seed from taking root. These opposing forces are also present today, and they hinder the process of planting biblical stewardship principles in the lives of stewards.

We are tempted to fight against these forces, which is just what the evil one wants us to do, because in doing so, we lose our focus. Our role is to sow truth. The best way to help the soils, or souls, is to reveal these opposing forces for what they really are by teaching biblical truths so that people are not deceived.

Let's look at the dark spiritual forces at work. The evil one in the text of Mark 4:15 is out to "take away the Word that was sown in them." Put simply, Satan is snatching the seed we are sowing. So what are we to do? Keep sowing as much seed as possible, because on many soils the seed won't be snatched; it will take root, sprout and bear fruit.

Practically speaking, ministry leaders need to shift from occasionally talking about stewardship to talking about it all the time. We need to integrate a philosophy of holistic biblical stewardship in everything we do, allowing the light of God's Word to shine.

In the book, *How to Increase Giving in Your Church*, George Barna demonstrated through his research that people appreciate biblical instruction about their spiritual responsibilities and relationship with God and money.

> As I studied the best fund-raising churches in the nation, it was obvious that the practical, no-holds-barred preaching and

teaching of biblical principles of stewardship, and relentlessly holding the body of believers accountable to those truths in appropriate ways, were cherished distinctives of these families of Christians devoted to growing even in the difficult, sacrificial aspects of the faith.[15]

Sowing principles is shining the light of the Word of God in people's lives. Light dispels darkness. Holding believers accountable is encouraging them to walk in the light, helping them discern truth from lies.

Material possessions can also stifle the seed planting process in spring. Mark 4:19 reads, "the deceitfulness of wealth and the desires for other things come in and choke the word, making it unfruitful." It is possible for people to hear truth but be so wrapped up in their pursuit of possessions that they miss the message.

Rick Warren spoke of this temptation in his popular book, *The Purpose-Driven Life.*

> Money has the greatest potential to replace God in your life. More people are sidetracked from serving by materialism than by anything else. They say, "After I achieve my financial goals, I'm going to serve God." That is a foolish decision they will regret for eternity. When Jesus is your Master, money serves you, but if money is your master, you become its slave.[16]

What makes wealth so deceitful is that it can be used to accomplish so many purposes that it tricks people into seeking after it and hoarding it. In so doing, even noble saints become enslaved.

Other dangers to avoid in today's media-driven environment may be social or cultural in nature. The evil one bombards us with messages about the cares of the world and every believer must discern how those messages are inconsistent with the Word of God. If we don't, we will be assimilated into the cultural norms. Here are a few examples.

Most advertising about money embraces the notion that life is about possessions. This belief was also prevalent at the time of Christ—He clearly spoke out against it in Luke 12:13-21. Taken to an extreme, this notion leads one to hoard in an attempt at financial security.

So how much is enough? How much wealth can secure a person's future? John D. Rockefeller answered, "One more dollar." If he could never attain it, why would we try?

This thinking has infiltrated the Church today. In teaching His disciples how to pray, Jesus said to ask God for daily bread. Do we do that today? Or do we plan the rest of our lives through *responsible financial planning*? Regarding money, Jesus said to store it up in heaven through giving. What do we do? We give a portion but demonstrate our trust is in our own ability *by having savings and retirement accounts to secure our financial future.* Jesus celebrated giving that was sacrificial, such as the widow of Mark 12:41- 44, who gave all she had.

When was the last time you heard about someone giving away all they had to live on?

The dangers during the sowing season are many. The evil one is snatching the truth out of hearts, so we must sow it often and abundantly. The good things of this world distract us. Without realizing it, we handle wealth like the rest of the world, because the worldly messages have made such a powerful impression. The result in many cases is that biblical stewardship principles neither take root nor do they result in stewards who are rich toward God.

Despite the dangers, if we sow abundantly and if we spread truth about money as frequently as Jesus did, some of it will take root and bear fruit. We have Jesus' word on it!

Summary: Don't let the dangers in the sowing season distract or defeat you in the planting process. Keep sowing!

6. Tips for Nurturing Seedlings

Any farmer knows that there are a lot of factors that hinder the healthy growth of seed in fertile soil. Lack of water, sunlight, hail, and flooding, to name some that are out of the control of the sower. What the sower can do is to continue to sow wherever he touches soil and broadcast seed to the entire field through crop dusting techniques.

The Christian leader must focus on nurturing each person through personal interaction and correspondence, caring more about spiritual preparation than the giving. The leader must also send encouragement through mass communications to nurture the whole community along the same lines.

Face-to-face visits scatter the seeds of truth. Therefore the Christian leader should make as many contacts with people as possible. But how does a leader approach this important work? Those you call may shrink from appointments because they think you are calling to ask for money. Be persistent and soon people will realize you are not trying to get anything from them, but rather inviting them to be a part of God's work in a variety of ways.

Take a Geritol approach to nurturing individual givers. Years ago, Geritol marketed the effectiveness of their product based on a daily dose; *it* was the "one-a-day" vitamin. If the ministry you serve has 250 givers, work through the list over the course of a year, about 250 working days. Call one giver per day. For most, one quick phone call or email sets up a personal visit. For geographically dispersed givers, the call may be the only contact you can make. If your list is larger than 250, divide it and get help from fellow staff members.

More challenging is if you have thousands of givers; you cannot possibly meet with all of them. Instead, coordinate multiple media channels, such as email blasts, to communicate messages you would share in person. Think of it as crop dusting.

When calling on someone, regardless of his or her connection to the ministry, approach with intentionality. Say you are calling to set up a meeting to hear what God is doing in their life and to share what God is doing at the ministry. Use these five P's to remember the purpose of each visit.

1. **Person** – Learn about who they are, not just what they do.

2. **Passion** – Find out what facet of God's work they are passionate about.

3. **Permission** – Seek permission to share about your ministry.

4. **Participation** – Share how stewards participate in the King's work.

5. **Pray** – Encourage them to pray about their response.

For some, this approach could be interpreted as disingenuous or merely a spiritual tactic to get at their wallet. Patience is the best way to demonstrate that you care more about people and their growing faith than the amount of their giving, and what you are really offering is the opportunity to join God in His work through different forms of partnership and participation.

Practice this and you will find that givers will grow to trust and respect you; they will see you are truly seeking to help them grow in Christ.

This is about discipline. How often does the important work of nurturing seedlings get squeezed out by the tyranny of the urgent? Too often! Meetings, crisis situations, and surprises hit our calendars each day, and then days become weeks. If we have not disciplined ourselves to be sure to call one constituent per day, we probably will not have sown much seed by the end of the year. And if we don't sow, what will we reap? When we do call, the result is a calendar full of appointments and more stewards engaged in the King's business.

Encouraging spiritual growth in many people's lives is a bit more challenging to facilitate, but there are some great resources to help you. Books like *The Treasure Principle* by Randy Alcorn, *The 40 Day Spiritual Journey to a More Generous Life* by Brian Kluth, *Fields of Gold* by Andy Stanley, and *Generosity: A Four Week Devotional* by Gordon MacDonald are four good examples in addition to the *NIV Stewardship Study Bible.* Each of these books will take you on a spiritual journey to bring growth in your personal understanding and practice of stewardship, and they are great for sharing with large groups of people.

Many ministries have distributed these resources by mail or at events, and have reaped abundantly. Encouraging spiritual growth in constituents has resulted in dramatically higher levels of giving, prayer support and volunteer service. Remember, you are sowing seed to produce a crop thirty-, sixty-, one-hundredfold. Sow resources like these—or develop one of your own—and see what happens.

***Summary:** Help seedlings grow not by seeking anything from them but by giving them what they need to thrive.*

The Season for Cultivating the Souls — Summer

"The teaching of stewardship is actually the making of faithful disciples of Jesus Christ."[17]

⌐ *Charles Cloughen, Jr.* ⌐

Summer is the season when farmers do what they can to cultivate the plants, though God makes them grow. At this time in the growth cycle, the sower must look at the fields, attentive to the needs of different plants. Of course, this is in addition to the regular care crops need. Since a farmer will need more workers to help him cultivate their growth, summer is the season for finding co-laborers.

Applied to raising Kingdom resources, this section of this spiritual almanac will provide you with three tools: a lens for looking at the fields, attentive to cultivating a variety of stewards; insight on caring for the crop by evaluating how your communication may help or hurt the growth of the stewards in your care; and advice for finding co-laborers who can help you encourage Christian generosity.

| Seasonal Overview: The Work of the Sower in Summer ||
Secular Fundraising	Biblical Steward-raising
7. Leaders manipulate givers through moves management to get them to make gifts to the organization.	7. Leaders leave the giving results up to God. They try to discern where people are in their stewardship journey to encourage them to grow in the grace of giving.
8. Leaders communicate with the ultimate goal of getting something from people.	8. Leaders communicate with the goal of imparting something to people.
9. Leaders encourage people to join them to accomplish their purposes.	9. Leaders seek to engage others to get involved in God's work in community.

Figure 3. The third season: nurturing growth.

7. Look at the Fields

A farmer can grow different crops, and each requires different kinds of care to become fruitful. For instance, some require water daily while others survive a week between drinks. Some plants blossom in full sun, others in dappled light. Corn, wheat, barley, oats, rice, and soybeans all have different needs. Just as an almanac answers questions related to these crops, this section of the book answers them in relationship to people.

If you want to help people grow in their spiritual understanding and practice of biblical stewardship, you need to look at the fields to see what is there. In practical terms, this means you have to ask questions. Basic questions help you discern what motivates people. *Do you give to your local church? What other organizations do you support financially? What motivates you to give so faithfully?* Ask these not to manipulate, but to meet people where they are and encourage them in their growth. Remember, Jesus was unashamed to talk about giving as He "sat down opposite the place where the offerings were put," in Mark 12:41-44, in order to teach his disciples the difference between giving out of one's surplus and giving sacrificially. He was not timid talking about money and giving, and neither should we be. Jesus loved asking questions, not because He did not know the answers, but to get people to think.

On the secular side, asking questions is also a common practice. For instance, in their book *The Seven Faces of Philanthropy*, Prince and File researched the motivations of 476 people who had given at least $25,000 annually to charity.[18] They concluded that there were seven types of answers to the why question: *Why have you given so much money to this organization annually?*

The seven motivations they discovered were: (1) the Communitarian, (2) the Devout, (3) the Investor, (4) the Socialite, (5) the Altruist, (6) the Repayer, and (7) the Dynast. By recgnizing the seven faces, they could learn to communicate in ways consistent with donors' motivators to move them to give. That process is often guided by a secular concept called moves management.

There are different examples of moves management cycles in secular fundraising, but essentially each of them seek to move names through these basic stages: (1) identify, (2) qualify, (3) cultivate, (4) solicit, and (5) steward.

In looking at the fields, should Christian leaders seek to understand giving motivations and handle lists of names using moves management techniques? The answer is yes and no.

Asking questions to discern giving motivations is great, but to do so with the goal of manipulating people is not leaving the results up to God. But asking questions to get to know people so that you will interact with them in a way that works according to their needs is consistent with biblical concepts.

This is what it might look like at your ministry. For the Communitarians, outline how their giving can transform the community. For the Devout, point them to examples of faithful stewards in the Scriptures. For the Investors around you, provide the numbers, which will help them think of ways to leverage their giving for maximum Kingdom return. For the Socialites in your midst, host events to encourage participation with the ministry in community. For the Altruists, engage them at whatever level of involvement makes them comfortable. For the Repayer, show how participation can, in turn, bless others. And for the Dynast, show them how leaders like Barnabas in the books of Acts fueled the work of ministry by leading the way with generous giving.

As for moves management, should you steward the relationships in your care as CEO or pastor of your church? Absolutely. The key here is to lead people toward transformation rather than merely making transactions. Don't manage relationships to accomplish your ends. Rather encourage people to discern how the Holy Spirit is leading them in their lives. Again, ask questions to facilitate these discoveries.

In his book, *God and Your Stuff: The Vital Link Between Your Possessions and Your Soul*,[19] Wesley K. Willmer evaluated the "Correlation of Soul Maturity and Use of Possessions." His chart (page 61) helps leaders use what we learn from asking questions to grow themselves and help others grow in the grace of giving.

As you ask questions related to money and giving, people's answers will tell you where they are in the relationship between their faith and their possessions. If they appear to give with no intentionality or regularity but rather in response to emotional appeals for support, they may be at the Imitator stage in Willmer's chart. People who give sporadically and out of duty to others tend to be in the Modeler stage. Those at the Conformer stage see their giving as an obligation and though giving more consistently, it is probably out of their surplus and not sacrificial.

Correlation of Soul Maturity and Use of Possessions

Stages	Faith Characteristics	Evidence in Use of Possessions
Stage 1: **Imitator**	Like a child, is marked by imagination and influenced by stories and examples of others.	Is able to mimic the examples of others in giving when shown or instructed.
Stage 2: **Modeler**	Takes beliefs and moral rules literally. Perception of God is largely formed by friends.	Gives sporadically when given an example to follow.
Stage 3: **Conformer**	Faith becomes a basis for love, acceptance, and identity; involves most aspects of life and is shaped mainly by relationships. Faith does not yet form a cohesive "philosophy of life."	Gives because it is the thing to do. Likes recognition, tax benefits, and other personal gain from giving.
Stage 4: **Individual**	Begins to "own" one's faith. Faith is less defined by others as one becomes able to personally examine and question one's beliefs.	Starts to give in proportion to what God has given. Danger of becoming prideful regarding giving or giving for the wrong motives. Wonders why others do not give more.
Stage 5: **Generous Giver**	Grasps the main ideas of an individualized faith as well as individual practices. Becomes interested in developing the faith of others.	Recognizes that all one owns is from God. Begins to give of one's own initiative, rather than out of obligation or routine. Derives joy from giving.
Stage 6: **Mature Steward**	Little regard for self. Focuses on God and then on others. Free from manmade rules.	Recognizes the role of a faithful steward of God's possessions. More concerned with treasures in heaven than on earth. Content with daily provision.

Figure 5. The Stages of Giving from Wesley K. Willmer's book *God and Your Stuff: The Vital Link Between Your Possessions and Your Soul.*

Somewhere between stage three and stage four of Willmer's chart, transformation starts to happen. And, if we are asking questions to move people toward transformation, as this chart illustrates, our interactions should encourage them toward becoming a mature steward.

For those who like to see this process visually, consider another chart from *God and Your Stuff*.[20]

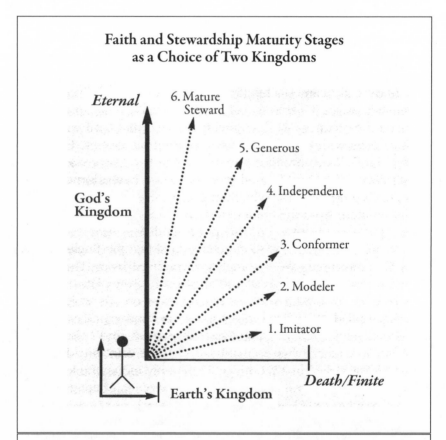

Faith and Stewardship Maturity Stages as a Choice of Two Kingdoms

Eternal

6. Mature Steward

5. Generous

God's Kingdom

4. Independent

3. Conformer

2. Modeler

1. Imitator

Death/Finite

Earth's Kingdom

Figure 6. The stages of transformation, from Wesley K. Willmer's book *God and Your Stuff: The Vital Link Between Your Possessions and Your Soul.*

Notice that giving in stages one through three ultimately only focuses on earthly objectives. Imitating, modeling and conforming behavior are external actions, which like the sacrifices of God's people in the Old Testament, are meaningless to God without a transformed heart. As you ask questions, if you discern that people are giving with an earthly focus, encourage them to raise their sights heavenward.

At stage four, notice that the trajectory of an individual's giving moves from the earthly kingdom to God's Kingdom. Proportionate giving begins to take place here, though pride is the trap that thwarts many from moving on toward maturity. Stage five stewards are Generous Givers. Their giving is motivated by joy rather than obligation and sacrificial compared to their resources. At the top of the chart, the Mature Steward is the kind of person who demonstrates an increasing attachment to God and seeks to invest all they are and all they have to advance His purposes. Regardless of their level of wealth, Mature Stewards become increasingly detached from possessions, they exhibit contentment with whatever they do have and can be found giving gratitude to God for all their blessings, both material and immaterial.

Ask questions and consider how the responses you receive fit in these stages; then ensure your interaction encourages spiritual growth. Do this to help each giver become rich toward God. Just as different crops have different needs, the community of faith needs its leaders to look at the fields, ask questions and respond with attentiveness and intentionality. The point is not to provide the same care for everyone but to be attentive and responsive to the particular needs of each one.

For large groups of people, a leader must resist the temptation to forego the vital cultivation work. Still, it is necessary to nurture spiritual growth in each life. This can be done by persistently weaving biblical stewardship principles into all communications, remaining aware of different motivations. In so doing, at different rates and in different ways, you will help all grow in the grace of giving.

Summary: *Ask questions and listen to people's answers to discern how best to help them grow in the grace of giving.*

8. Care for your Crops

Besides what plants need specifically, farmers must provide general care
in summer. This general care is best summed up as *communication*.

What messages about generosity are you sending in your direct mail?
Is every gift and every giver valued equally despite the differences in
their capacity and propensity to give? How do you proclaim your
values through your institution's magazine or church newsletter?
Are those who give more celebrated in the community over those
who give smaller gifts?

What difference does this make?

If you don't provide general care for your crops through careful
communication, you limit your harvest at best. Financially, it can
mean the difference between exceeding a campaign goal and having
a stalled or even failed attempt.

How does a leader communicate so that the messages encourage
generosity? It must be done with clarity, without favoritism, and
without expecting anything in return. Communication consistent with
biblical principles results in Spirit-led transformation in people's lives.
However, communication with favoritism or expectations is secular
moves management at work. This is a very large pitfall to avoid.

Every leader is tempted to approach wealthy people differently due
to their greater resources. As Jesus taught in Mark 12, sacrificial giving
comes from sources you least expect. James concurs in chapter 2,
reminding readers not to show favoritism within the body of Christ.
The bottom line is: resist the tendency to give extra attention to the
wealthy. Still, we must realize that they are often among the most
abused people in the community of faith. Paradoxically, you may
need to minister to them.

Henri Nouwen addressed this issue in the *Spirituality of Fundraising*.
He cites the story of a very rich woman who felt worthless because of

the way she was treated. Listen to the pain from her heart: "You know, Henri, everybody is after my money. I was born into wealth and my family is wealthy. That's part of who I am, but that's not all there is. I am so afraid that I am loved only because of my money and not because of who I really am." [21] Nouwen goes on to help us realize that "we must minister to the rich from our own place of wealth— the spiritual wealth we have inherited as brothers and sisters of Jesus Christ." [22]

An alternate path to take, whether the person is wealthy or not, is to inquire sincerely about that person's relationship with Jesus. When a development officer asked a celebrity about his walk with Jesus, the man replied, "No one has ever asked me that question." The measure of success with all communication should not be the size of the gift; but rather, does the interaction draw him or her closer to Jesus? Incidentally, the celebrity gave a large gift saying the interaction drew him closer to God and God motivated him to give more than he had planned.

The purpose of your communication with individuals is to find out where they are on the journey and encourage growth in faith. God takes care of the results, because as people conform to the image of Christ, Who is generous, they become more generous themselves. Your job is to encourage them along that path through communication.

Many ministry leaders are also tempted to do prospect research to qualify the giving capacity of constituents. Should they? Before answering, consider Jesus' words to His disciples when He sent them to minister in His name (Luke 10:1-7).

> After this the Lord appointed seventy-two others and sent them two by two ahead of him to every town and place where he was about to go. He told them, "The harvest is plentiful, but the workers are few. Ask the Lord of the harvest, therefore, to send out workers into his harvest field. Go! I am sending you out like lambs among wolves. Do not take a purse or bag or sandals; and

do not greet anyone on the road. When you enter a house, first say, 'Peace to this house.' If a man of peace is there, your peace will rest on him; if not, it will return to you. Stay in that house, eating and drinking whatever they give you, for the worker deserves his wages. Do not move around from house to house."

Notice that when Jesus sent the disciples out, he did not urge them to identify and qualify prospects and to lean on the wealthy to fund God's work. He sent them on a faith journey. They trusted solely in Him to open people's hearts and homes to them. Jesus also sent them forth with confidence that He would work through receptive people to provide for their needs.

In the ministry of raising Kingdom resources, God wants leaders to look for receptive people, not rich people. That's the danger of prospect research. It presupposes that you will favor people who are rich because of what you might get from them. No wonder rich people like the woman Henri Nouwen cited feel abused.

So, should a leader do prospect research? Well, yes and no.

In traditional prospect research, you determine *capacity* first. *Capacity* means estimating a person's holdings by means of public record. Next you would cultivate relationships with them to get large gifts for your organization.

For the stewardship officer, understanding *capacity* is certainly a useful tool. However, it must *not* be used to show special treatment for the wealthy, as is the temptation but rather to identify a good starting point for conversation and discerning a prospect's needs rather than viewing them as the answer to meeting yours. And capacity is only half the research that can be done. *Propensity* is another characteristic to analyze. *Propensity* can be defined as identifying those God has inclined to give to ministries like the one you serve.[23]

For instance, if you identify a foundation that supports ministries in California that are like yours, and your organization is in Colorado, a call might reveal that though your missions are aligned, God has worked in the heart of the founders to support only ministries in that state. In another example, a foundation supports a specific sector of ministry all over the country. If you serve in that field, a call might result in an invitation to send a proposal. These examples illustrate determining propensity and help the ministry leader find people whose hearts already resonate with the same ministry focus.

In researching *capacity* and *propensity*, you must use what you find to help you accomplish your work effectively without giving special treatment to specific people, because as Jesus taught, sacrificial giving comes from where you least expect it.

Besides communication with individuals, the sower can also use mass communication, mindful that what you celebrate says what you value. Does your ministry share stories only when huge gifts are received? If so, what message are you sending to monthly givers about how you value their partnership with you?

How about the frequency of your communication? One consultant instructed a ministry leader to send at least sixteen letters a year seeking support or else suffer a dramatic drop in giving. Later, a survey of those constituents revealed that they felt that all the ministry wanted was their money. Is that the impact you want to have? Certainly not! Your leadership must determine how your practice aligns with your beliefs. Might people actually give more if treated differently? What would a communications audit uncover?

Two more examples of caring for your crops are relevant. One ministry sent weekly prayer emails during a three-year building campaign. They were short and to the point. The goal was to encourage deeper faith as God worked through the campaign. By the end, people actually asked for the emails to continue, saying that those devotional thoughts really blessed them spiritually.

The other example falls in the realm of asking for volunteer service. An urban ministry reported more than 10,000 hours of volunteer service in the first year of formally engaging volunteers, and that contributed to its ability to double the ministry capacity. When asked, they expressed that God raised up the army of workers; all they had done was share the ways people could serve.

If, in the sowing season of spring, our desire is to plant seeds in people's lives that will invite their holistic participation in God's work, then in the cultivation season of summer, we should make it easy for them to partner with us in those ways.

Summary: *Careful communication nurtures growth by affirming the stewardship messages you are communicating to your people.*

9. Find Co-laborers

Farmers rally all the help they can get for harvest time and so should you. In an agrarian setting, every farm hand is put to work because there is so much to do. How does a Christian leader rally such assistance? Because the harvest is plentiful and the laborers are few, your job is to ask God to send workers to help, and He often brings people alongside to join you even as you are ministering to them.

Let's say God has given you a passion for ministering to the homeless through a rescue mission and you want others to join you. How can you go about engaging others? Create venues for your constituents to introduce their friends to your mission. For location-based ministries such as rescue missions, these are *point-of-entry* events.[24] They create a point of entry to introduce guests to your organization over a breakfast, lunch, coffee, dinner or dessert. Food is always a great catalyst to bring people together. For ministries without a specific location, get people together in the home of a board member and share stories of those touched by the organization. And when everyone is gathered strategically, do not seek a gift but raise their sights to God, to how He may have them participate in a variety of ways.

As the leader of a ministry, you want to help board members get more involved, so have an orientation process for new trustees and educate them through good books regarding fiduciary, strategic and generative governance roles. Provide them with clear talking points and encourage them to memorize the mission so they can share it wherever they go.

In addition to orienting and educating board members, ask them to give you "six moments of time" each year.[25] Through "six moments of time," trustees are asked to be strategically supportive by hosting events like a dinner to introduce the president to friends; coffee with the stewardship officer and a friend; sponsoring and filling a foursome in the charity golf tournament; bringing guests to an upcoming point-of-entry event and so forth. By asking for "six moments of time," you are making it easy for board members, as well as other volunteers, to directly assist in expanding your organizational community. Does your organization make it easy for people to work alongside you?

Again in the words of Henri Nouwen, "I wonder how many churches and charitable organizations realize that community is one of the greatest gifts they have to offer."[26] To invite people to serve, sharing that privilege, is one of the greatest gifts we can give, because it is not our ministry, but God's work.

Summary: Make it easy for people to join you in sowing their time, energy and resources at the ministry you serve.

The Season for Reaping the Harvest — Fall

"May it please His Majesty
that the extraordinary generosity
He has shown this miserable sinner
serve to encourage and rouse those who read this
to abandon completely everything for God.
If His Majesty repays so fully that even in this life
the reward and gain possessed by those who serve Him
is clearly seen,
what will this reward be in the next life?" [27]

⌐ *St. Teresa of Avila* ⌐

We have the privilege of serving as stewards of His majesty. He has generously blessed us to be a blessing to others, and that truth summarizes our work in the preceding seasons of the sower. In the fall, we will see fruit from our labors, and we can also anticipate but hardly fathom the reward that awaits us for our faithfulness.

Fall is the season for reaping the harvest. The laborers are in place, ready to assist. The fields are bursting with yield. The law of the harvest says that if you have sown generously, you will reap abundantly. So with joy, go reap your results!

In this concluding section, sowers will be challenged to measure ministry results rather than merely monetary results—again shifting the focus to what we can control, rather than what we cannot control. Sowers also have faith in God's abundance while urging all stewards to deploy the resources God has put in their care with generosity. Finally, the culmination of our work must be to celebrate His provision with thankfulness.

Seasonal Overview: The Work of the Sower in Fall	
Secular Fundraising	**Biblical Steward-raising**
10. Leaders rely on their own efforts and measure success in monetary terms.	10. Leaders trust God to provide and set spiritual or ministry goals.
11. Leaders' perception is fear-based; in a scarcity mentality they compete for limited resources from givers.	11. Leaders see through the lens of faith so an abundance mentality allows them to co-labor rather than compete.
12. Leaders celebrate what people have done and give them glory.	12. Leaders celebrate God's provision and give glory to Him.

Figure 7. The fourth season: harvest equals provision.

10. Set Spiritual Goals and Reap Abundantly

If you have sown biblical stewardship principles in people's lives, you will reap a harvest thirty-, sixty-, or one-hundredfold. Jesus said so. Receiving financial gifts means reaping the results of sowing biblical truths. However, a great harvest is not always measured monetarily.

Leaders may consider shifting from monetary goals to ministry goals. Making this shift requires a change in measurement. Believing you are the fundraiser means you can only measure monetary goals. If you believe that God is the Fundraiser and you are a sower, you will measure ministry-related activities. In other words, if the results are up to God, then measure the activities that can be expected of a stewardship officer.

Rather than counting money, count the number of personal visits, phone calls and other personal correspondence you have with givers and potential new friends. Instead of totaling the amount from a fundraising event, set goals for using events to expose your mission to a specific number of people. In place of a solely monetary goal for planned gifts, consider as your goal a certain number of personal messages using different media channels. Like the sower who strategically sows his fields, you want to measure activities that encourage spiritual stewardship decisions. To choose not to would be like a farmer choosing to do nothing all year—no planting, no cultivating, no irrigating, nothing. How preposterous it would be to expect a bumper crop at harvest time. Yet many ministry leaders do exactly that when it comes to encouraging Christian generosity.

If your only measurement of success has been financial each year, discuss a new set of goals with your supervisor. The job of the stewardship officer is to do the right things consistently and trust God with the results. Do the job of a sower in the first three seasons, and the financial targets will take care of themselves in the fall. Projects will get funded—some from expected sources and some from sources you did not expect. You will exceed annual fund targets in the same way. But more importantly, each year the harvest will exceed your expectations because stewardship seeds were sown. Where God gives the vision, He provides the provision.

Summary: When you reap generously, count not only the money God provided, but see what other ministry goals were more than met.

11. Have Faith in Unlimited Abundance

A farmer's almanac often projects the size of the harvest through calculations of factors that impact the harvest. Weather patterns, precipitation projections, and temperature trends can all influence the harvest. In the same way, spiritual, social, and global factors influence giving trends. Since tough economic times breed a scarcity mentality, people must be encouraged to make decisions rooted in faith rather than in fear.[28] In challenging economic times, the Bible offers countercultural messages for three kinds of stewards.

The first message is for people who act as steward over a storehouse, overseeing the distribution of the assets of a foundation. What is the temptation in an economic crisis? Hoarding, right? In Genesis 41, in a time of catastrophic famine, Joseph's response was not to hoard but to open the storehouses! Joseph shared freely what God had provided in seasons of plenty.

This example has touched a number of foundation executives, causing them to shift their philosophical approach from giving a standard five percent each year to giving more in difficult years and less in boom years. The tax code allows them to carry forward—up to five years—the amount they give over five percent in a boom year to cover future years when they may give less than five percent. Essentially, the challenge is to exhort those with seed in times of famine to sow it and many are responding!

The second message is for those who possess a portfolio of assets. The biblical role model for them is Barnabas. When the apostles had needs, Acts 4:36-37 tells us that he sold one of his assets, a tract of land. He did not sell all his land, just a portion of it.

Many stewards today have portfolios of stock, real estate, and other marketable securities. In down economies, brokers or financial advisors advise their clients to hold onto assets. Ministry leaders can remind those with portfolios that selling some of what they have is an avenue to giving that is open to them even in difficult times.

One steward owned a number of apartment complexes and, after much prayer, concluded that he should sell one and give the proceeds to a ministry. Sure enough, it sold the same day he listed it. He promptly donated the proceeds, realizing that in lean financial times, he had resources to share.

The third biblical message applies to all other stewards: give generously to God. Follow the examples of the widow of Zarephath from 1 Kings 17 in the Old Testament or the Macedonians of 2 Corinthians 8 in the New Testament. Regardless how much you have, give generously to

God. The giving in these two examples went beyond capacity, flowing from a place of unswerving trust in God.

These are the examples we must use with our constituents in difficult times. They don't make sense in terms of secular philanthropy, but the point of this approach is to help people see how to use their resources consistent with Scriptural examples, mindful that stewardship decisions are based on what one does have.

Here is another consideraton. Some experts say to ask for a specific gift, others say you should not, and some recommend asking for a multi-year commitment. So what should the leader do?

Even as not all givers are the same, neither are all asks the same. An ask is a request for financial support, intended to result in a desired response. Secular fundraising theory calls for closing a gift transaction by suggesting a specific amount. Jesus taught us that sacrificial giving often comes from sources we least expect, so perhaps we should let givers tell us how much they are led to give.

As for the giving commitment, recent trends indicate asking for three-, four- or even five-year commitments to maximize the time of the asker. These commitments free the asker to expand the support base without having to call on every constituent every year. Tough financial times lead many to stop making multi-year commitments. So what should the leader do?

By now, you probably know the answer: the approach will be different for each person. For those with inconsistent or sporadic income, multi-year annual giving may be appropriate. For those who live on a salary, a multi-year monthly commitment may be in order. Because stewardship decisions are based on what one has and not on what one does not have,[29] generally giving will probably follow suit. Follow the leading of the Spirit in requesting Kingdom resources.

Summary: Don't try to control the participation process. Ask people to give in a manner that makes sense with all that God has called them to steward.

12. Celebrate with Thanksgiving

For generations, the American celebration of the culmination of harvest is the Thanksgiving feast. At that time, the laborers' work is done, the harvest has been bountiful and portions have been distributed to all who share in the experience. And, each year in the farmer's almanac, there are tips for cooking up an unforgettable Thanksgiving event.

In the same way, this spiritual almanac must end with instructions for a harvest celebration that will joyfully give praise and thanks to God. In 2 Corinthians 9:12-13, Paul said this about giving:

> This service that you perform is not only supplying the needs of God's people but is also overflowing in many expressions of thanks to God. Because of the service by which you have proved yourselves, men will praise God for the obedience that accompanies your confession of the gospel of Christ, and for your generosity in sharing with them and with everyone else.

How we celebrate says clearly Who we believe is actually doing the fundraising. If we celebrate as Paul did, we help people realize that their generosity not only shows the depth of their faith, but gives glory to God. Is this happening in your home, at your church or ministry? If you want it to, maybe it is time for you to become a sower.

Summary: When the Kingdom of God is advanced through His people's generosity, there is no doubt that God accomplished the work and God receives the glory.

Postscript

The second section of this book came full circle back to where it started—where my life started—sowing seeds. My family owned a greenhouse business, Hoag's Greenhouses, which operated for 82 years. We grew tomatoes and cucumbers. For more than a decade, I learned how to do everything from planting seedlings to driving the truck to market.

My favorite place was the growth chamber, a twenty-by-forty foot room with six stadium lights in it. You had to wear sunglasses to go in. As a child I thought it was heaven, it was so bright in there. Hundreds of thousands of seeds were planted in that room.

One by one, with tender loving care, workers planted seeds in holes no more than an inch wide filled with rich soil. With the right amount of light and water, they would sprout in a few days and then were transplanted into larger containers. Eventually they were planted in our greenhouse, a five-acre, climate-controlled glass facility. With irrigation, fertilization, nutrient-feeding, lots of hard work and much prayer over a few months, a harvest would come. I could not believe how many tomatoes or cucumbers came from each plant.

Then—and now—the only way to reap a huge harvest was to sow abundantly. We invested in sowing all our time, energy and resources. To this day I have not stopped sowing. I invite you to join the revolution in generosity that flows from sowing seed, rather than picking "low-hanging" fruit.

Through the four seasons of this spiritual almanac, the objective has been to provide you with practical advice for sowing transformational stewardship principles based on a solid theological foundation to help people become mature stewards who are rich toward God.

We trust you found this book to be useful. If so, please share it with someone else, but do not stop there. Consider your constituency to be the growth chamber. Carefully, take your seed and sow it in as many lives as you can. As growth becomes evident, do what you can to nurture it and ask God to produce a harvest beyond your wildest dreams.

> "Remember this: Whoever sows sparingly will also reap sparingly, and whoever sows generously will also reap generously." [30]

Almanac Summary at a Glance

Seasonal Overview: The Work of the Sower in Winter

Secular Fundraising	Biblical Steward-raising
1. Leaders consider their role as being the *fundraisers* for the organization.	1. Leaders understand their role is to sow biblical stewardship principles; God is *the Fundraiser*.
2. Leaders strategize to get people to make gifts to their organizations.	2. Leaders gather biblical truths that encourage people to become givers who are rich toward God.
3. Leaders do whatever works to get people to respond generously.	3. Leaders model generosity and pray for God to help people grow spiritually in the grace of giving.

Seasonal Overview: The Work of the Sower in Spring

Secular Fundraising	Biblical Steward-raising
4. Leaders seek transactions: gifts to accomplish their organizations' purposes from donors who have financial resources.	4. Leaders seek transformation: to help others use the spiritual and material gifts entrusted to them to accomplish God's work.
5. Leaders reinforce worldly thinking through strategies such as public donor recognition that may work culturally but be inconsistent biblically.	5. Leaders help people discern between worldly thinking and godly thinking by modeling biblical stewardship principles.
6. "It's all about relationships!" The leader's goal is to build relationships with people that will result in many gifts over many years.	6. "It's all about the most important relationship!" The leader's goal is to draw people closer to God. As a result they will be more generously involved in God's work.

Seasonal Overview: The Work of the Sower in Summer	
Secular Fundraising	**Biblical Steward-raising**
7. Leaders manipulate givers through moves management to get them to make gifts to the organization.	7. Leaders leave the giving results up to God. They try to discern where people are in their stewardship journey to encourage them to grow in the grace of giving.
8. Leaders communicate with the ultimate goal of getting something from people.	8. Leaders communicate with the goal of imparting something to people.
9. Leaders encourage people to join them to accomplish their purposes.	9. Leaders seek to engage others to get involved in God's work in community.

Seasonal Overview: The Work of the Sower in Fall	
Secular Fundraising	**Biblical Steward-raising**
10. Leaders rely on their own efforts and measure success in monetary terms.	10. Leaders trust God to provide and set spiritual or ministry goals.
11. Leaders' perception is fear-based; in a scarcity mentality they compete for limited resources from givers.	11. Leaders see through the lens of faith so an abundance mentality allows them to co-labor rather than compete.
12. Leaders celebrate what people have done and give them glory.	12. Leaders celebrate God's provision and give glory to Him.

Biblical Principles for Stewardship and Fundraising

Christian leaders, including development staff, who believe in the Gospel of Jesus Christ and choose prayerfully to pursue eternal Kingdom values, will seek to identify the sacred Kingdom resources of God's economy within these parameters:[1]

1 God, the creator and sustainer of all things and the One "Who works within us to accomplish far more than we can ask or imagine," is a God of infinite abundance and grace.[2]

2 Acknowledging the primacy of the Gospel as our chief treasure, Christians are called to lives of stewardship as managers of all that God has entrusted to them.[3]

3 A Christian's attitude toward possessions on earth is important to God, and there is a vital link between how believers utilize earthly possessions (as investments in God's Kingdom) and the eternal rewards that believers receive.[4]

4 God entrusts possessions to Christians and holds them accountable for their use, as a tool to grow God's eternal Kingdom, as a test of the believer's faithfulness to God, and as a trademark that their lives reflect Christ's values.[5]

5 From God's abounding grace, Christians' giving reflects their gratitude for what God has provided and involves growing in an intimate faith relationship with Christ as Lord of their lives.[6]

6 Because giving is a worshipful, obedient act of returning to God from what has been provided, Christian fundraisers should hold a conviction that, in partnership with the church, they have an important role in the spiritual maturation of believers.[7]

7 The primary role of a Christian fundraiser is to advance and facilitate a believer's faith in and worship of God through a Christ-centered understanding of stewardship that is solidly grounded on Scripture.[8]

8 Recognizing it is the work of the Holy Spirit that prompts Christians to give (often through fundraising techniques), fundraisers and/or organizations must never manipulate or violate their sacred trust with ministry partners.[9]

9 An eternal, God-centered worldview promotes cooperation rather than competition among organizations, and places the giver's relationship to God above the ministry's agenda.[10]

10 In our materialistic, self-centered culture, Christian leaders should acknowledge that there is a great deal of unclear thinking about possessions, even among believers, and that an eternal Kingdom perspective will often seem like foolish nonsense to those who rely on earthly kingdom worldview techniques.[11]

When these principles are implemented, which rely on God changing hearts more than on human methods, the resulting joy-filled generosity of believers will fully fund God's work here on earth.[12]

---

[1] Mt. 6:19-21; Mt. 6:33

[2] Gen. 1; Ps. 24:1; Col. 1:17; Eph. 3:20; Ps. 50:10-12; Phil. 4:19; 2 Cor. 9:8; Jn. 1:14; Heb. 1:3

[3] Rom. 1:16; 1 Cor. 9:23; Phil. 3:8-11; Mt. 13:44; Mt. 25:14-46; 1 Pet. 4:10; 1 Cor. 1:18; 1 Cor. 1:23-24; Mt. 28:18-20; Gen. 1:26-30

[4] Mt. 6:24; Mt. 22:37; 1 Tim. 6: 6-10; Phil. 4:17; Mt. 19:16-30; Lk. 14:12-14; 1 Cor. 3; 2 Cor. 5:10; Eph. 2:10; 1 Tim. 6:17-19; Mt. 25:31-46

5 Lk. 16:1-9; Lev. 19:9-10; Deut. 14:22-29; Deut. 24:19-22; Is. 58:6-7; Gal. 2:10; 1 Cor. 16:1; 1 Cor. 9:14; 2 Cor. 8:14-15; 2 Cor. 9:12; Jas. 2:15-16; Heb. 13:15-16; 1 Tim. 6:17-19; Mal. 3:10; Mt. 6:24-33; Lk. 12:15-34; Mt. 25:14-46; Eph. 2:10; Jn. 15:8-10; Jn. 15:12-17; Jn. 13:34-35; Mt. 22:34-40; 2 Cor. 8-9; Gal. 6:10; Col. 3:17; 1 Tim. 6:18

6 Mk. 12:41-44; Lk. 12:16-34; Gen. 14:20; Ezr. 2:69; Lk. 7:36-50; 2 Cor. 9:10-12

7 1 Chron. 29:10-14; Rom. 12:1; Jas. 3:1

8 2 Tim. 3:16-17; Ex. 34:32; Ex. 35:21

9 Jn. 15:4-5; Is. 32:15-17; Is. 34:16; Jn. 15:16-17; Jn. 15:26; Jn. 16:13-14; Jn. 6:63; Jn. 14:15-21; 1 Thes. 1:2-6; 1 Thes. 2:13; Gal. 5:16-25; Rom. 12:4-8; 1 Pet. 1:2; Neh. 1:4-2:8; Is. 55:8-11; 2 Cor. 9:5-7; 1 Chron. 28:6; 1 Chron. 29:9; Prov. 21:1; 2 Cor. 3:5

10 2 Cor. 4:16-18; 1 Cor. 3:1-9; Phil. 4:7; Gal. 5:13-25; Ps. 90:1-12

11 1 Cor. 1:17-31; 1 Cor. 2:1-5; 1 Cor. 2:14

12 Ex. 36:6-7; Mt. 6:10; 2 Cor. 9:8-12

Endnotes

Shift from Transactions to Transformation

1 Peter Chrysologus (c. 380-450), *Sermon 22.*

Move from Two-Kingdom Bondage to One-Kingdom Freedom

2 Dwight Lyman Moody, *The Gospel Awakening* (Chicago: F.H. Revell, 1883), p. 276.

Focus on Cultivating Hearts that Will Joyously Become Stewards

3 Alan Gotthardt, *The Eternity Portfolio: A Practical Guide to Investing Your Money for Ultimate Results* (Wheaton: Tyndale House, 2003), p. 160.

Grow as a Sower

4 Richard Baxter (1615-1691), *The Reformed Pastor* (The Religious Tract Society: London, England, 1982), p. 77.

The Season of Preparation – Winter

5 Brennan Manning, *The Furious Longing of God* (Colorado Springs: David C. Cook, 2009), p. 120.

6 Jeavons, Thomas and Rebekah Birch Basinger, *Growing Givers' Hearts: Treating Fundraising as Ministry* (San Francisco: Jossey-Bass, 2000), p. 2.

7 See the Appendix B for the ECFA list of *Biblical Principles for Stewardship and Christian Fundraising.*

8 Visit www.stewardshipresourcebible.org for more information.

9 Henri Nouwen, *The Spirituality of Fundraising* (Richmond Hill, Ontario: Henri Nouwen Society, 2004), p. 11.

10 Nouwen, p. 23.

11 Lauren Tyler Wright, *Giving—the Sacred Art: Creating a Lifestyle of Generosity* (Woodstock, VT: SkyLight Paths Publishing, 2008), p. xxii-iii.

12 Wright, p. xxiii.

The Season for Sowing Seed — Spring

13 Richard Foster, *The Challenge of the Disciplined Life: Christian Reflections on Money, Sex & Power* (San Francisco: Harper Collins, 1985), p. 42.

[14] For a more in-depth explanation of the four I's, read pages 272-5 in *Revolution in Generosity,* edited by Wesley K. Willmer.

[15] George Barna, *How to Increase Giving in Your Church: A Practical Guide to the Sensitive Task of Raising Money for Your Church or Ministry* (Ventura, CA: Regal Books, 1997), p. 91.

[16] Rick Warren, *The Purpose-Driven Life: What on Earth Am I Here For?* (Grand Rapids: Zondervan, 2002), p. 267.

The Season for Cultivating the Souls — Summer

[17] Charles Cloughen, Jr., *One Minute Stewardship Sermons: Communicating the Stewardship Message Every Sunday of the Year* (Harrisburg, PA: Morehouse, 1997), p. xiv.

[18] For more information than is presented here, read: Russ Alan Prince and Karen Maru File, *The Seven Faces of Philanthropy: A New Approach to Cultivating Major Donors* (San Francisco: Jossey-Bass, 1994).

[19] Wesley K. Willmer, *God and Your Stuff: The Vital Link between Your Possessions and Your Soul* (Colorado Springs, CO: NavPress, 2002), p. 44-45.

[20] Willmer, p. 52.

[21] Nouwen, p. 18.

[22] Nouwen, p. 21.

[23] Read the chapter authored by Rich Haynie in *Revolution in Generosity*, and review the chart on page 95

[24] For more details on implementing this concept, read: Axelrod, Terry, *Raising More Money: A Step-by-Step Guide to Building Lifelong Donors* (Seattle: Raising More Money Publications, 2000).

[25] Wm. Edward Laity and David G. Lalka of DVA Navion have helped me implement this concept.

[26] Nouwen, p. 28.

The Season for Reaping the Harvest — Fall

[27] Teresa of Avila, *The Book of Her Life* (Indianapolis: Hackett, 2008), p. 138.

[28] See the *FOCUS on Accountability* article by Gary Hoag in Q1, 2009: www.ecfa.org/Content/FocusOnAccountability.aspx.

[29] 2 Corinthians 8:12.

[30] 2 Corinthians 9:6.

Other Related Resources

Alcorn, Randy, *Money, Possessions and Eternity* (Wheaton: Tyndale House, 2003).

Blomberg, Craig L., *Neither Poverty Nor Riches: A Biblical Theology of Possessions* (Downers Grove: InterVarsity Press, 2001).

Frank, John R., *The Ministry of Development* (Woodinville: Steward Publishing, 2005).

Jeavons, Thomas and Rebekah Burch Basinger, *Growing Givers' Hearts: Treating Fundraising as Ministry* (San Francisco: Jossey-Bass, 2000).

Kluth, Brian, *40 Day Spiritual Journey to a More Generous Life* (Available online at www.kluth.org).

MacDonald, Gordon, *Secrets of the Generous Life: Reflections to Awaken the Spirit and Enrich the Soul* (Wheaton: Tyndale House, 2002).

MacDonald, Gordon with Patrick Johnson, *Generosity: Moving Toward Life that is Truly Life* (Alpharetta: The National Christian Foundation, 2009).

Nouwen, Henri J.M., *The Spirituality of Fundraising* (Richmond Hill, Ontario: Henri Nouwen Society, 2004).

Rodin, R. Scott, *Stewards in the Kingdom: A Theology of Life in All Its Fullness* (Downers Grove: InterVarsity Press, 2000).

Rodin, R. Scott, *The Seven Deadly Sins of Christian Fundraising* (Spokane: Kingdom Life Publishing, 2007)

Stanley, Andy, *Fields of Gold: A Place Beyond Your Deepest Fears: A Prize Beyond Your Wildest Imagination* (Wheaton: Tyndale, 2004).

Stott, John R.W., *Stott on Stewardship: Ten Principles of Christian Giving* (Chattanooga: Generous Giving. 2003).

Willmer, Wesley K., *God and Your Stuff: The Vital Link Between Your Possessions and Your Soul* (Colorado Springs: NavPress, 2002).

Willmer, Wesley K. ed., *Revolution in Generosity: Transforming Stewards to Be Rich Toward God* (Chicago: Moody, 2008).

Vincent, Mark L., *A Christian View of Money: Celebrating God's Generosity* (Eugene, Oregon: Wipf & Stock, 2007).

Featured Website

www.SowerBook.org

Related Websites

www.ECFA.org

www.GenerosityMonk.com

www.GodandYourStuff.org

www.OneAccordPartners.com/NFP

www.RevolutioninGenerosity.org

Other Related Resources

www.RevolutionInGenerosity.org

Other Related Resources

www.GodandYourStuff.org